D1505330

TONI MORRISON

LUCILLE P. FULTZ

Toni Morrison

Playing with Difference

UNIVERSITY OF ILLINOIS PRESS

URBANA AND CHICAGO

© 2003 by the Board of Trustees of
the University of Illinois
All rights reserved
Manufactured in the United States of America
C 5 4 3 2 1
∞ This book is printed on acid-free paper.

Library of Congress
Cataloging-in-Publication Data
Fultz, Lucille P.
Toni Morrison : playing with difference /
Lucille P. Fultz.
p. cm.
Includes bibliographical references and index.
ISBN 0-252-02823-6 (acid-free paper)
1. Morrison, Toni—Criticism and interpretation.
2. Difference (Psychology) in literature.
3. Race in literature. I. Title.
PS3563.08749Z64   2003
813'.54—dc21   2002015034

Contents

Acknowledgments

I am grateful to the Division of Humanities and the Department of English at Rice University for time and support in completing this project. I acknowledge the encouragement and invaluable support of students and colleagues, most especially the late Joe Austin, James M. Cox, Carolyn Denard, Ann T. Diggs, Andrea Doughtie, Ed Doughtie, Linda Driskill, Nellie Y. McKay, Marilyn Mobley McKenzie, Katheryn P. Thomas, and Cherrigale Townsend.

Toni Morrison: Playing with Difference owes much to the insightful comments of those who read portions of the manuscript: Saundra Y. Boyd, John F. Callahan, Audrey Y. Crawford, Terrence Doody, Helena R. Michie, David Minter, Carol Quillen, Esta Seaton, Robert B. Stepto, and Katharine Wallingford.

I also wish to thank Donald E. Pease and Robyn Wiegman for the opportunity to discuss portions of chapter 2 with cohorts in the Back to the Futures Summer Seminar at Dartmouth College; the staff at Rice University Fondren Library; and Julie Grob, director of Special Collections, the University of Houston M. D. Anderson Library.

For assistance with copyediting and phrasing, I am particularly grateful to Terry Munisteri, amanuensis extraordinaire. In addition, I would like to express my appreciation for the clerical help of Jamie Cook and Lanita Martin; the technical computer expertise and aid of Carolynne White, Steve Iltis, and Chesson Olawaiye; and the research assistance of Nadeen Agour.

This book owes much to the keen and professional eyes of Theresa

L. Sears, managing editor at the University of Illinois Press, and Dawn Hall, my copy editor. I would also like to thank the anonymous readers, whose rigor and insights helped me sharpen my arguments, and Willis G. Regier, director of the Press and my editor, for his belief in the merits of this book and for his understanding and encouragement through the long, hard hours.

Toni Morrison Chronology

1931 Born 18 February in Lorain, Ohio, to Ella Ramah (Willis)
and George Wofford, and given the name Chloe Ardelia
Wofford.

1949 Graduated from Lorain High School with honors.

1953 Graduated from Howard University with B.A. in English.
Changed her middle name from Ardelia to Anthony while
at Howard; thereafter was known as "Toni."

1955 Graduated from Cornell University with M.A. in English.

1955–57 Appointed English instructor, Texas Southern University.

1957–64 Appointed English instructor, Howard University.

1958–64 Married to Harold Morrison. Couple had two sons, Harold
Ford and Slade Kevin.

1964 Divorced Harold Morrison and returned to Lorain, Ohio.

1965–67 Hired as senior editor at Random House in its textbook
subsidiary, L. W. Singer Publishing, Syracuse, New York.

1967 Moved to Random House's New York City headquarters as
senior editor.

1970 Published *The Bluest Eye*, her first novel.

1971–72 Appointed associate professor of English, State University
of New York, Purchase.

1973 Published *Sula*, her second novel.

1974 Edited *The Black Book*.

1975 *Sula* nominated for National Book Award.
Received Ohioana Book Award for *Sula*.

1976–77 Appointed visiting lecturer at Yale.

1977   Published *Song of Solomon,* her third novel.
            Song of Solomon chosen as Book-of-the-Month Club's main
            selection.
            Received the National Book Critics Circle Award and the
            American Academy and Institute of Arts and Letters Award
            for *Song of Solomon.*
1978   Chosen as subject of PBS series *Writers in America.*
            Received the Cleveland Arts Prize for one "who [has]
            brought distinction to herself and renown to the city of
            Cleveland."
1980   Appointed to National Council on the Arts.
1981   Published *Tar Baby,* her fourth novel.
            Appointed to American Academy and Institute of the Arts.
            Featured on cover of *Newsweek* magazine.
1983   Published "Recitatif," a short story.
1984   Retired from Random House.
1984–89   Appointed Albert Schweitzer Professor of Humanities,
            State University of New York, Albany.
            Received the New York State Governor's Arts Award.
1986   *Dreaming Emmett* (unpublished drama), commissioned by
            the New York State Writers Institute, performed by Mar-
            ketplace Repertory Theater of Albany.
1986–88   Appointed visiting professor at Bard College.
1987   Published *Beloved,* her fifth novel.
            Received the first Washington College Literary Award.
            Appointed lecturer at the University of California, Berke-
            ley.
            Nominated for National Book Award and National Book
            Critics Circle Award for *Beloved.*
            Beloved selected by Book-of-the-Month Club as its main
            feature.
            Appointed Regents' Lecturer at University of California,
            Berkeley, and Santagata Lecturer at Bowdoin College.
1988   Received Pulitzer Prize, Robert F. Kennedy Award, and Be-
            fore Columbus Foundation Award for *Beloved.*
            Forty-eight black writers and critics published a letter in
            the *New York Times* registering their protest that *Beloved*
            did not receive the National Book Award.
            Received the Elizabeth Cady Stanton Award of the Nation-
            al Organization of Women.
1989   Received the Modern Language Association of America's

Commonwealth Award in Literature.

Appointed Robert F. Goheen Professor of Humanities, Princeton.

1990   Appointed Clarke Lecturer at Trinity College, Cambridge.

Delivered the William E. Massey Lectures at Harvard.

Received the Chianti Ruffino Antico Fattore International Literary Prize.

1992   Published *Jazz,* her sixth novel; *Playing in the Dark: Whiteness and the Literary Imagination;* and edited *Race-ing Justice, En-Gendering Power: Essays on Anita Hill, Clarence Thomas, and the Construction of Social Reality.*

Appeared on the *New York Times* Best-Seller List for fiction and nonfiction.

1993   Wrote lyrics to *Honey and Rue,* a song cycle set to music by André Previn, which premiered in Chicago.

Toni Morrison Society founded in Baltimore, Maryland.

Awarded the Nobel Prize in literature.

Delivered the Nobel Prize lecture and acceptance speech.

Her house on the Hudson River in New York destroyed by fire in December.

Stamp honoring Toni Morrison issued by the Swedish Academy.

1994   Received the Rhegium Juli Prize for Literature, the Pearl Buck Award, and the Condorcet Medal and held Condorcet Chair, Paris.

1995   Signed charter of the Toni Morrison Society, Atlanta, Georgia.

Teamed with Max Roach and Bill T. Jones for performance of "Degga," a dance/musical/narrative piece, at Lincoln Center for the Performing Arts.

1996   Delivered the twenty-fifth Jefferson Lecture.

Received the National Book Award for Distinguished Contribution to American Letters.

Song of Solomon discussed on the *Oprah Winfrey Show.*

1997   Edited with Claudia Brodsky Lacour *Birth of Nation'hood: Gaze, Script, and Spectacle in the O. J. Simpson Case.*

1998   Published *Paradise,* her seventh novel.

Paradise discussed on the *Oprah Winfrey Show.*

First Biennial Conference of the Toni Morrison Society, "Toni Morrison and the American South," held in Atlanta.

Motion picture *Beloved* debuted in October.

1999   Coauthored with Slade Morrison *The Big Box.*
        "Envisioning Paradise: A Conference on Toni Morrison's
        Art and Imagination," Princeton, sponsored by the Program
        in African American Studies.
2000   Second Biennial Conference of the Toni Morrison Society,
        "Toni Morrison and the Meanings of Home," held in Lo-
        rain, Ohio.
        The Bluest Eye discussed on the *Oprah Winfrey Show.*
        Awarded the National Humanities Medal.
2001   Toni Morrison Society celebrated Morrison's seventieth
        birthday in New York City.
2002   *Sula* discussed on the *Oprah Winfrey Show.*
        Honored by National Council of Women of the U.S.A., Inc.

Sources: Sharon Malinowski, ed., *Black Writers: A Selection of Sketches from Contemporary Authors,* 2d ed. (Detroit, Mich.: Gale Research, 1994), 431–39; Toni Morrison Society Web site, <http://www.gsu.edu/~wwwtms/index.html>, 19 February 2002; and Lorain County, Ohio, Public Library Web site, <http://www.lorain.lib.oh.us/localauthors/morrison_chronology.html>, 19 February 2002.

TONI MORRISON

1   *"Who Will Play with Jane?":*
Toni Morrison's Invitation
to Her Readers

> I have to provide the places and spaces so that the reader
> can participate. Because it is the affective and participa-
> tory relationship between the artist and the speaker and
> the audience that is of primary importance.
> —Toni Morrison, "Rootedness"

For more than thirty years, Toni Morrison has been commenting on her fiction and narrative strategies. She has stated that her writing
is a cocreation between author and reader. While this notion of fiction as
a shared process is not new, what is striking is Morrison's unfailing vision of this cooperative venture as indisputably integral to all her fiction.
I trace Morrison's search for appropriate structures to recreate the multivalent experiences of African Americans as marginalized individuals in
American society in general and within the African American community in particular and the ways in which one society impacts the other.

Between the publication of *Sula* (1973) and *Paradise* (1998), Morrison eloquently spoke and wrote about the relationship between her writing and her race, between the way she writes and what she chooses to
write about. In 1974, for example, she spoke of her desire for critics who
could see the interrelatedness between artistic merit and politics, for
critics who could "put together the inseparable qualities of greatness and
politics" (Taylor-Guthrie 4). Morrison's critique of critical practices as
they related to African American literature in the United States during

the turbulent 1960s and 1970s points toward what she felt was the need for a different perspective on the role of writing by African Americans and a new direction for African American criticism. She argued for criticism that would engage literature by African Americans within relevant critical practices and not merely as a sociological study of black life. While the sociological is relevant, indeed essential to any engagement with African American life, Morrison urges that it cannot be the end of criticism and theory. Rather, she argues, the sociological informs, de rigueur, African American art, but it must do so within the context of a given artistic construct.

Although Morrison has been consistent in asserting the reader's responsibility in the construction of her fictional texts, she has, over time, changed her politics about race and gender differences. This Emersonian political shift—"Speak what you think now in hard words, and to-morrow speak what to-morrow thinks in hard words again" (McQuade 1:1148)— is one measure of Morrison's developing sensibility as a woman and as an artist. Two examples immediately come to mind. In 1974, Morrison cautiously spoke of what she considered to be "a male consciousness" and "a female consciousness" as totally separate spheres. She then stated, "Black men—and this may be way off the wall because I haven't had time to fully reflect about this—frequently are reacting to a lot more external pressures than Black women are. For one thing they have an enormous responsibility to be *men*." Morrison went on to reinforce her conviction: "All I'm saying is that the root of a man's sensibilities [is] different from a woman's" (Taylor-Guthrie 7). Morrison slightly modified this view when she spoke of her construction of Sula as a rebel, a masculinized figure, and an equal partner in sexual relations in the 1920s and 1930s. She stated that Sula did not depict "a typical black woman at all" (Stepto, "Intimate Things" 219).[1] In fact, the narrator of *Sula* tells us that Sula's personality was a combination of her grandmother's "arrogance" and her mother's "self-indulgence . . . with a twist that was all [Sula's] own imagination" (118). In *Sula*, Morrison chooses sexual intercourse as one occasion to represent this "very atypical" black woman and to show that with Ajax Sula realizes that "sex was not one person killing the other." In order to achieve this parity in heterosexual intercourse, Morrison "pictured [Sula] on top of [Ajax] . . . like a tree [because] he was secure enough and free enough and bright enough" to see Sula as "a whole person, not as an extension of himself" (220). The interesting turn in Morrison's comment on this scene of gender parity is her focus on Ajax's freedom as a kind of rebellion against notions of manhood that allows him to accept Sula as equal rather than to stress—as the novel does—Sula's refusal to be the traditional woman.

What is absent from Morrison's analysis of this scene is a discussion of Sula's agency. What, other than Morrison's description of the inversion of Sula's position during sexual intercourse, makes her a nontraditional woman since the focus is on Ajax's security in his manhood? Sula, after experiencing orgasm with Ajax, over time becomes not the liberated woman but the stereotypical female standing in front of a mirror "trying to decide whether she was good-looking or not" and "tying a green ribbon in her hair," having already prepared the bathroom, bedroom, and "set [the table] for two" (*Sula* 131–32).

Morrison's early discussions about and play with gender differences are later stated in more complex and complicated constructions of difference. She speaks of Sula's and Cholly Breedlove's "lawlessness" in her first two novels, but by the time she publishes *Tar Baby* (1981) and *Paradise*, she has radically altered her views on freedom and individualism. She celebrates and challenges Jadine's freedom to abandon her black roots, and later, in *Paradise*, she questions a group of African Americans' decision to use their color (racial "purity") as a sign of group loyalty and as an excuse for gender oppression.

Morrison similarly modifies her views on African Americans' attitude regarding evil. In *Sula*, she writes that the community could accommodate Sula as the embodiment of evil because "there was no creature too ungodly as to make them destroy it." If there was evil in their midst, it was "something to be first recognized, then dealt with, survived, outwitted, triumphed over" (118). In 1974, again speaking about Sula, Morrison stated that "Black people never annihilate evil. They don't run it out of their neighborhoods, chop it up, or burn it up, they don't have witch hangings. They accept it. It's almost a fourth dimension in their lives. . . . they don't have that puritanical thing which says if you see a witch, then burn it, or if you see something, then kill it" (Taylor-Guthrie 8). Morrison revises this point of view within the black community in *Beloved* when the thirty women, through prayer and song, led by Ella, expel the "devil-child" who had "taken the shape of a pregnant woman" (261). This moment of concerted female power releases Sethe from Beloved's oppression: "It broke over Sethe and she trembled like the baptized in its wash" (261), while Beloved is left "Alone. Again" (262) and "Disremembered" (274). Some ten years later in *Paradise*, Morrison radically revises her views on black communal tolerance of evil incarnate. Morrison's shifting views about the tolerance of evil within the African

American community may be explained in part by shifting societal and cultural attitudes in the 1980s and 1990s. No doubt by the 1990s she was acutely aware of the effects of desegregation, integration, and economic opportunities on African American life and could therefore conceive of the possibility that African Americans would not only consider themselves "bewitched" but also deem it necessary, even feel "obliged[,] to stampede or kill" (3) a group of women they perceive to be the source of evil encroaching on their community. But Morrison's depiction of a group of women exorcizing from their midst a woman who they believed—as evidenced by Sethe's condition—was causing irreparable harm to Sethe is markedly different from the actions of a group of men taking violent actions against women about whom they have manufactured evidence of evil. Contrast this moment with the reference to mob violence in *Sula:* "They [the black community] could kill easily if provoked to anger, but not by design, which explained why they could not 'mob kill' anyone. To do so was not only unnatural, it was undignified" (118). Morrison is clearly critiquing and condemning white mob violence as she underscores the ostensibly justifiable violence that erupts in African American communities. In one sense, if we consider narrative time—1939 in *Sula* and 1976 in *Paradise*—Morrison was thinking not so much about her own time—authorial time—as she was about black communal attitudes relative to events covered in her discrete texts.

However we choose to think about time in Morrison's fiction, the foregoing examples illustrate Morrison's changing attitudes about gender and race and also speak to her willingness to bring her readers into her development. A self-conscious and self-reflexive writer, Morrison, in constructing her later novels, surely was aware that her readers could and, no doubt, would refer to her other fiction as they parsed meaning within and across her oeuvre. If one accepts this premise, then it is prudent to scrutinize closely recurring moments in which several narratives repeat, revise, and even contradict one another. Sometimes Morrison's fiction invites her readers to be directly and self-consciously involved in the writing; at other times she is more evasive, and readers may miss the writerly-readerly moment and attribute the confusion to Morrison's carelessness or lack of clarity. There is a scene in *Beloved* where three women's voices thematically become one. Structurally—until the point is clarified—the reader may be tempted to sort out the voices to determine which line is whose. It is evident when the dialogue begins that Denver is speaking, but as the questions and answers become more assertive and possessive, the speakers' identities become less certain.[2]

You are my Beloved
You are mine
You are mine
You are mine (216)

More than content is at issue here: Morrison is testing our readerly competence and insisting that we work to uncover meaning behind the construction of this scene. To lose sight of who is speaking is to become totally enmeshed in the narrative moment. But to step back and ask who is speaking and discover the indeterminacy of the speakers can lead from analysis of technique to interpretation. This dual project of analyzing narrative strategy and interpreting meaning is part of what I believe Morrison has in mind when she speaks of the reader's role in textual construction.

A different kind of authorial evasion occurs in *Sula* and appears as a blank—ten years of silence between 1927 and 1937. Nothing is written until Sula's ominous return to Medallion in 1937, "accompanied by a plague of robins" (89). Why does Morrison create this gaping hole? The answer is dispersed across the remainder of the novel. For example, when Nel asks Sula to tell her about "the big city. . . . The nightclubs, and parties," Sula's answer provides clues to some of her peregrinations: "I was in college, Nellie. No nightclubs on campus." Nel responds, "You wasn't in no college for—what—ten years now? And you didn't write to nobody. How come you never wrote?" (99). The answers to Nel's questions are the answers the reader is seeking as well. We later learn that Sula had returned to Medallion because she was bored with "Nashville, Detroit, New Orleans, New York, Philadelphia, Macon and San Diego" (120). Morrison tells Stepto that in *Sula* she was "trying to be provocative without using all of the traditional devices of provocation": "I think I know how to do it by simply relying an awful lot on what I believe the reader already knows. I wanted Sula to be missed by the reader. That's why she dies early. There's a lot of book after she dies. . . . I wanted them [readers] to miss her presence in that book as that town missed her presence" (Stepto, "Intimate Things" 218). Morrison might well have added that much had gone on in the town during Sula's ten-year absence, but without Sula's presence or some overt interest in her absence, the narrative is in stasis. So the reader is aware of Sula's absence only because the dates in the text signal her absence. Once that absence is signaled, the reader is prompted to wonder about Sula's whereabouts and activities during this period. Morrison risks this provocation and fills in the blanks as information about Sula's absence is solicited from other characters or as it becomes necessary to fill in gaps about Sula's life. Such omissions and evasions are quintessential Morrisonian gestures.

Morrison has admitted that she does not mind taking risks and that she enjoys "the danger in writing when you're right on the edge, when at any moment you can be maudlin, saccharine, grotesque, but somehow pull back from it, well, most of the time." In addition to "this emotional response" she wants an "intellectual response to the complex ideas" in her work. Toward these goals, she states that her responsibility is "to do both at the same time" since "that's what a real story is" (Ruas 97). Henry Louis Gates Jr. has described Morrison as "a subtle craftsperson and a compelling weaver of tales" and as "the most formally sophisticated novelist in the history of African-American literature" (Gates and Appiah x). It is precisely Morrison's subtle and challenging craft that attracts and fascinates many readers. I see myself as the reader[3] Morrison has in mind when she describes her craft as one that "appears solitary but needs another for its completion" (*Dancing Mind* 14). Her choice of the word "craft" has special resonance for me because it speaks directly to my concern: how to be a Morrison reader and yet maintain a critical distance; how to be an able partner in this symbiotic relationship while creating sufficient space between myself as reader and Morrison as writer to offer Morrison's readers critical and theoretical analyses that do not compromise my integrity or the integrity of the texts under scrutiny.

In this study I focus on what Morrison terms the "potency of difference" ("Race and Literature"). I examine the extent to which markers of difference influence Morrison's narrative decisions and how they enable and challenge readers' attempts to come to terms with her innovations. Gates has spoken of Morrison's chief attributes as her "ability to create densely lyrical narrative textures" that are singularly hers and "to make the African-American 'experience' the basis for a representation of humanity *tout court*" (Gates and Appiah xi). Since Morrison's fiction is historically determined, readers parsing her fiction must also concern themselves with synchronic and diachronic issues—namely, the time of publication of each work and the social and cultural events that generally concern society but are specifically relevant to African Americans. Although Morrison's fiction transcends the time and events narrated, these elements cannot be ignored. Readers must consider time, as represented in the discrete narratives, whether it be the time of slavery and postemancipation, of the various wars of the twentieth century and their attendant effects on African Americans' changing attitudes toward their civil rights, or of the 1920s and 1960s when African Americans' aesthetic sensibilities radically transformed their attitudes about themselves in relation to Western modes of representation. Morrison's retrieval of colonial New England witchcraft in *Paradise* makes a statement about alliances and intolerance within the African American community in the 1970s.

Morrison's first novel, *The Bluest Eye*, published at the height of the Black Aesthetics movement, calls into question the contemporaneous slogan "Black is beautiful" and challenges readers to consider the seeds of black self-hatred, the demons within black psyches, and the culprits within the broader culture that contribute to black low self-esteem. *Sula*, also published during the Black Aesthetics movement and on the crest of the Women's Rights movement, raises questions about black women's individuation and independence. It engages black women's limited but expanding choices such as marriage, motherhood, education—even the choice to reject family and community values. As bell hooks has pointed out, home has not always been a place where black women have found freedom; home sometimes fosters "estrangement and alienation" and therefore "is no longer just one place" (*Yearning* 148). Hence, an individual such as Sula becomes a roaming figure in search of a home in the world at large. Although she returns to Medallion, Sula becomes alienated and estranged from her best friend and her community.

Song of Solomon (1977) was published at a time when black males were asserting their "manhood" based on a model characterized by economic advancement and dominance. Although these black men were resistant to white male dominance, they consistently sought to dominate black women and subvert white power through violence. At the same time, black women were arguing for equality within the African American community. *Song of Solomon* asks, among other things, What is the power of money and what are its effects on a presumed cohesive family and a nationalistic black community? What is the role of women in African American cultural memory? *Song of Solomon* also asks, Who am I in relation to my progenitors and the dominant society?

With the publication of *Tar Baby* in 1981 and "Recitatif" in 1983, Morrison raised issues engaging middle-class black women whose education and personal achievements create tensions within and outside the black community. In these texts the stakes are higher and the risks greater because of broader opportunities and larger cracks in the economic spaces; both female protagonists are no longer restricted to a defined space—the black side of the track, so to speak. In fact, Twyla's world ("Recitatif") extends beyond the orphanage to an upper-middle-class community north of New York City, while Jadine's education and beauty propel her beyond the limited world of Baltimore and Philadelphia to Paris, to the cover and middle pages of a Parisian fashion magazine, and to the prospects of a white husband (*Tar Baby*).[4]

Beloved (1987), *Jazz* (1992), and *Paradise* (1998) invoke early and contemporary American and African American history. Morrison's later fiction plays off her earlier fiction and calls into question the African American community's struggles against racism; its ability to recognize and resolve the conflicts within that community; and its willingness to challenge class and gender formations within the black community.

This book examines the processes by which Morrison represents these thematic concerns and attempts to assess her achievements. In calling Morrison's narrative processes "playing," I intend to use the word in all its polysemy and wish to invoke its functional and semiotic uses as noun, verb, and signifier. In considering the word "playing" notionally and con-notatively as a verb, I see it in the context of "centering," "privileging," "staging," "tantalizing," "teasing." As a noun or nominalization, it evokes, for me, such terms as "action," "activation," "activity," "drama," "pro-cess." The term "playing" also points toward textual signifiers inviting readings that tend toward Morrison's performative acts as a writer and toward the texts in all their manifestations as "pawns" in the writer's hand. I am using "playing" as a narrative choice and a narrative act. These limited foci enable readings, at best, on three fields of play: the author's field of writing, the textual field of signification, and the reader's field of interpretation. I intend to offer a different way of reading and understand-ing Morrison's fictional texts as technical achievements and as models of storytelling.

My signal for these ways of reading emerges from Morrison's use of the term "playing" in *Playing in the Dark* (1992), in which she speaks about her approach to writing:

> I am interested in what prompts and makes possible this process of en-tering what one is estranged from—and in what disables the foray, for purposes of fiction, into corners of the consciousness held off and away from the reach of the writer's imagination. My work requires me to think about how free I can be as an African-American woman writer in my genderized, sexualized, wholly racialized world. . . . For me, imagining is not merely looking or looking at; nor is it taking oneself intact into the other. It is, for purposes of the work, *becoming*. (4)

Proceeding from Morrison's use of the term "playing," I would like to direct my reading toward selected moments in and methods by which she "plays" with(in) her fiction.

Because this study is concerned with aesthetic intention, it privileges not chronology but narrative technique. While this approach may seem redundant, it permits a fuller analysis of techniques employed in several texts. This analytical method can also reveal the extent to which Morrison manipulates language and characters in the service of art. I stress both aesthetics and ideology, intentions and themes.[5] This study is not intended to provide detailed analyses of specific texts. Rather it focuses on textual moments that best express aspects of Morrison's art.

Morrison's fiction constitutes a critique of race and racism in the United States—interrogating the black experience within and against a white ethos of dominance and resistance to change. As Morrison has stated, the body of her work is a "running commentary on race theory and cultural practice and how each shapes the other" ("Race and Literature"). She also views race as a metaphorical and political concept: "Race has become metaphorical—a way of referring to and disguising forces, events, classes, and expressions of social decay and economic divisions far more threatening to the body politic than biological 'race' ever was. . . . racism is as healthy today as it was during the Enlightenment. It . . . has assumed a metaphorical life so completely embedded in daily discourse that it is perhaps more necessary and more on display than ever before" (*Playing* 63). Given this preoccupation with race in life and literature, Morrison trains her fictional gaze on Africans—later, called African Americans—as they negotiate life in the United States and elsewhere, and she asks the question that is never satisfactorily answered: How can one be both black and free within a society that not only privileges white identity but also posits that identity as normative by denigrating and circumscribing blackness? Over a thirty-year period and through seven novels, one short story, one play, and a plethora of speeches and articles, Morrison leads us through the black geographical and psychological saga from Africa to and through America.

When asked if race informs her perspective as a writer, Morrison responded: "When I view the world, perceive it and write about it, it's the world of black people. It's not that I won't write about white people. I just know that when I'm trying to develop the various themes I write about, the people who best manifest those themes for me are the black people whom I *invent*. It's not deliberate or calculated or self-consciously black, because I recognize and despise the artificial black writing some writers do" (Tate 118; emphasis added). Morrison's decision to write from the site and perspective of her ethnicity is no less valid than Faulkner's decision to mine a small community (Yoknapatawpha County/Fayette County, Mississippi), his "little postage stamp of native soil" (Morris 313).

As Morrison puts it, even though Faulkner wrote "regional literature" it was "published all over the world," but "it is specifically about a particular world." Morrison adds, "That's what I wish to do" (LeClair 124). While embracing the centrality of her ethnicity to her writing, Morrison also suggests that her art transcends phenotypes and melanin and foregrounds language and personal knowledge. Morrison states elsewhere that, because the "discussion of black literature in critical terms is unfailingly sociology and almost never art criticism, it is important to me to shed those considerations from my work at the outset" ("Memory" 386). Kwame Anthony Appiah correctly notes that when race becomes the overarching issue in African American literature it can sometimes becloud criticism and theory relative to that literature ("Conservation of 'Race'" 37). Although Morrison's texts explore the dialectics of the socially and racially constituted self, these texts are first and foremost artistic constructions by a writer who consciously seeks to transform ideology into art. It is that power of Morrison's art to transform experience that, no doubt, accounts ultimately for the broad application of her ideas and discursive strategies.

Morrison's fiction engages the complexities and varieties of African American experiences and the best modes of representation for these experiences. Morrison articulates this view when she asserts that "writing and reading are not all that distinct for a writer. Both exercises require being alert and ready for unaccountable beauty, for the intricateness or simple elegance of the writer's imagination, for the world that imagination evokes" (*Playing* xi). Deborah Ayer Sitter, commenting on *Beloved*, encapsulates some of Morrison's self-conscious approach to narrative construction. "To sensitize her readers to alternative world views," Sitter writes, "Morrison uses a variety of structural and stylistic devices which expand the context so that characters' motives and actions acquire new meanings." Sitter also calls attention to Morrison's use of a narrative point of view that requires not just close reading but a suspension of judgment until all facts are revealed (20).

The imperatives of difference—such as race, class, gender, and physicality, with all their concomitant baggage—are central issues in Morrison's fiction. It is now time to ask some fundamental questions about Morrison's narrative aesthetics and her representations of these vexed issues. What narrative choices does Morrison make in constructing her fiction? How do the oppositional/collaborative and enigmatic voices who narrate certain texts help us to understand Morrison's aesthetics? Does her narrative play provide clues to some deeper aspects of the stories narrated and the characters whose lives engage us? Morrison's fictions—

within the context of their serious content and self-conscious engagement with the pathos and tragedy of black life—nevertheless, reveal a sense of play that does not undercut those deeply serious concerns. Rather, they provide fresh and dramatic disruptions that set up alternative readings and interpretations.

Nothing is simplistic in Morrison's fictional molding of black life. Her art is deliberate and deceptively accessible; it is, as Gates observes, "at once difficult and popular." While these "densely lyrical narrative texture[s]" may be "recognizable" (Gates and Appiah x–xi),[6] their intricate constructions are not necessarily apparent or readily understood. When they are closely scrutinized, however, these texts yield valuable insights into Morrison's politics and poetics. Morrison has stated that she would like "to interest people who are fastidious about reading" and admits that she occasionally "play[s] to the gallery"; because such readers are "valuable to me[,] I am never sure that what they find 'wonderful' in it isn't really what is valuable about it" (LeClair 123).

Consider *Jazz*, a novel in which Morrison melds a unique African American invention (jazz) and a received Western art form (the novel), through which she narrates and riffs on African American life. But the novel invites attention because it purports to speak in its own voice as *a novel*. Or consider *Paradise*, in which she brings together many of the issues she represents discretely in preceding works: gender, family, community, disruption, internalized racism, intolerance, among others. In *Paradise*, Morrison's representation of community is radically different from her earlier depictions: it is a community splintered not by white racism but by intraracial caste based on color and gender, and a community further diminished by intolerance based on fear of a women-centered enclave.[7] It is the reverse in *Sula*, where Sula's behavior is cause for gossip and innuendo but never enough for the community to force her to leave town. These stories reflect both the conditions and the struggles of African Americans as they attempt to deflect their gaze from others' derisive scrutiny and from what Frantz Fanon calls "collective autodestruction" (*Wretched* 54) in order to attain self-fulfillment through the creation of an all-embracing and supportive community. W. E. B. Du Bois's *The Souls of Black Folk* speaks of "a world that yields [African Americans] no true self-consciousness" but rather "a peculiar sensation . . . a sense of always looking at [themselves] through the eyes of a world that looks on in amused contempt and pity" (11). Morrison averts this refractive gaze toward an interior gaze that compels African Americans to confront themselves as both beautiful and flawed individuals with a capacity to mend and move forward.

Morrison's narrative choices open up a repertoire of cultural problems and an array of individual and communal efforts directed toward their solutions. That these decisions reflect long-standing narrative concerns for Morrison is made evident by our ability to locate them in her first novel, *The Bluest Eye,* and trace them throughout her published works. Yet Morrison continues to grapple with these issues as she searches for new modes of constructing and representing the African American community's ways of looking at itself as a distinct culture within the United States. To this extent, Morrison's texts reveal complex, sometimes daunting, but always exciting approaches to narrative.[8] Her texts feature multivalent perspectives and authorial strategies. Inge Crosman Wimmers formulates these perspectives from the reader's point of view as "multiple, interlocking frames of reference [that] account for the complex, interdependent nature of the various frameworks—cultural, textual, personal—within which a given reading takes place" (xv).[9] Morrison's fiction stages dialectics between and among disparate narrative voices, from different points of view and different sensibilities, providing varied responses to the same situations.[10] These texts begin with certain assumptions: that Morrison's readers are aware of the history and culture of African Americans and that they recognize a dichotomy between fictionalized events and characters and the real world that engenders and informs her fictional worlds. Although she orients her texts toward the African American experiences, Morrison is always conscious of a white presence—be it marginal or central.[11] By this I mean the actual presence of or interactions between blacks and whites and/or the indirect presence of whites through material culture or vestiges of white oppression. *The Bluest Eye,* for example, begins with a primer from the Western canon of early childhood education that establishes the grounds of aesthetic conflicts between the African American community and the larger white world and of the self-hatred that such a primer—and mass culture in general—inculcates in black psyches. *The Bluest Eye* posits such a dialectical and dichotomous framework, which may account for what Rachel Lee terms Morrison's desire to "cultivate an aesthetic of ambiguity" (571).

Morrison further reminds us that the African American community is not an isolated community by alerting us to subtle and concrete evidence that the white community is never too far away. In *Paradise* we are repeatedly reminded that the white community is ninety miles from Ruby. Frequently, it is the pervasive awareness of white society, often marginal in its physical presence, that has a profound effect on the internal affairs of the African American community. In *Sula* much of what happens in the Bottom is controlled largely by decisions made by entities in the white community of Medallion and in the nation at large: the Bottom itself came into existence because of a white man's joke and unfairness toward his black slave; Shadrack is shell-shocked as a result of his service in the United States Army during World War I; the storming of the tunnel and the resulting deaths of many blacks are due to the white community's refusal to employ blacks in the construction of that abandoned tunnel. These examples of racism evidence Morrison's revelation of how black psyches may be ravaged by racist practices. At the core of these figurations of racism is Morrison's ongoing search for forms that suggest possibilities for countering racism and repairing African Americans' bruised psyches and bodies and recovering their sometimes rejected and often forgotten past.

Beyond its aesthetic function, this ambiguity underscores Morrison's desire to dispel any notion of a monolithic voice within the African American community or within her oeuvre. This ambiguity reminds readers of the multidimensionality of the African American community and the multiple angles from which Morrison approaches this community. Aware of the tremendous burdens and limiting possibilities for African Americans engendered by white society, Morrison reminds us that African Americans themselves must assume some responsibility for their own self-hatred. She neither excuses nor averts our gaze from the "seamy" underside of black America. Nothing is too horrible for depiction or too painful for words when we consider Eva's murder of her son Plum (*Sula*) or Violet's mutilation of a corpse (*Jazz*).[12] The details are vividly portrayed, not for sensationalism but to enable our understanding of the forces that cause certain individuals to engage in such heinous behavior while others, like Sula, can unwincingly gaze upon such tragedies. More important, Morrison demands that we see the whole picture—including the unspeakable. She, therefore, by design privileges the negative in the African American community. Black characters subjected to white influence are conflicted by their blackness, which they view as negative—as in *The Bluest Eye, Tar Baby,* and *Paradise.* In *Beloved* slavery and its effects are far too complex to render in a linear, mimetic narrative, and so Morrison moves between past and present, between consciousness and unconsciousness. As Barbara Hill Rigney observes, Morrison "scatters her signs, her political insights," thus demanding rigorous analyses of her "language" for readers willing to "reconstruct an idea of the political and artistic revolution constituted in her work" (7).[13]

Morrison's texts also disclose their relationship to and interplay with events "inside" and "outside" their constructed worlds. To this extent, her fiction delineates relationships between the world of the text and the external world of reality.[14] What Larry McCaffery says of Gabriel García Márquez's *One Hundred Years of Solitude* is equally applicable to Morrison's fiction. McCaffery notes that *One Hundred Years* "has . . . become a kind of model for the contemporary writer, being self-conscious about its literary heritage and about the limits of mimesis . . . yet managing to reconnect its readers to the world outside the page" (qtd. in Hutcheon, *Poetics of Postmodernism* 5). Morrison's texts, in their mimetic functions, tell us not so much what is but rather what is possible. As representations of race memory, these texts tell of the pains and the joys of African American experiences, which, according to Tom Feelings, "build on each other." To discuss pain without discussing the joys would be delimiting and questionable. As Feelings articulates it, "The more we learn about ourselves [as African Americans], the better we are able to connect with our ancestors."[15] And, as Paul Ricoeur puts it, "To narrate a story is already to 'reflect upon' the event narrated" (*Time and Narrative* 2:61). Ricoeur's assertion grows out of his own argument about the purpose and function of narrative: "We tell stories because in the last analysis human lives need and merit being narrated." This function of narrative, Ricoeur further states, evolves from the "necessity to save the history of the defeated and the lost" (*Time and Narrative* 1:75),[16] a major concern in Morrison's fiction.

The central queries Morrison makes are instructive to critics for reading not only her texts but African American texts in general. By using her own texts as models for aesthetic analysis, Morrison expresses her desire to have them subjected to the same rigorous scrutiny as that given to any text in the Western canon. She begins her analysis by orienting readers' attention toward "the question of what constitutes the art of a black writer, for whom that modifier is more search than fact, has some urgency." She then asks, "Other than melanin and subject matter, what, in fact, may make me a black writer? Other than ethnicity—what is going on in my work that makes me believe it is demonstrably inseparable from a cultural specificity that is Afro-American?" ("Unspeakable Things" 19). What connections can readers make between their life worlds and the worlds of Morrison's fiction? The answers to these questions are contingent on modes of reading.

Speaking with Elissa Schappell about the mechanics of her writing, Morrison states, "I work very hard in subsequent revisions to remove the writerliness from it, to give it a combination of lyrical, standard and colloquial language, to pull all these things together into something that I think is much more alive, and representative" (89). On the surface, Morrison's statement seems to be contradictory if we contemplate her use of the terms "invent" and "representative." These terms suggest her concern with "invention" and "writerliness," the process by which she constructs participatory fiction. For Morrison, there is urgency in creating this interplay between author and reader: "Having at my disposal only the letters of the alphabet and some punctuation, I have to provide the places and spaces so that the reader can participate" ("Rootedness" 341). She compares this relationship—the call and response—between author and reader to the relationship between a black preacher and his congregation. This collaborative enterprise accords the reader the status of observer/participant and allows her/him to "co-construct" these "writerly texts" (Barthes 5).[17] Morrison has stated that this process of writing is both "piecemeal and very slow" and that, unlike the successful advancement of an argument, her narration requires the active complicity of a reader willing to step outside established boundaries of the racial imaginary. Unlike visual media, "narrative has no pictures to ease the difficulty of that step" ("Home" 8–9). Gayl Jones expresses this theory of the reader's role when her narrator in *Mosquito* admonishes her readers that if she has not "described something" her readers "wants [sic] described, they be describing it they ownselves, and be composers they ownself" (94).[18] Following Jones's advice, I hope to provide the "pictures" and "descriptions" to further illuminate Morrison's fiction.

One compelling aspect of Morrison's writing is her ability to engage in the kind of narrative play that exposes *conceptions* as *misconceptions*. Her texts also indicate that her project is not merely to expose such misconceptions but to allow us the intellectual pleasure of uncovering meanings and intentions by alerting us to *clues* and *mis-clues* in a given text. The most salient but little known example of what I mean by "conceptions" and "misconceptions" and "clues" and "mis-clues" is Morrison's short story "Recitatif." This rarely discussed narrative contains all the elements of what I hope to bring to the attention of Morrison's scholars: the metanarrative processes Morrison employs to engage her readers in the reconstruction of the African American lifeworld. In other words, in "Recitatif" Morrison constructs a narrative about the writing and reading processes. In this story Morrison reveals her strategy of withholding information to engage readers actively in her writerly process and give them the rewards of close reading.

Morrison's narrative techniques develop from the obvious and seemingly facile play of perspective, focus, and voice in *The Bluest Eye* to the subtle and radical transformation of these narrative practices in her later works.[19] The transformation of these narrative voices in the service of her own discourse signals Morrison's development as a writer unwilling to settle for univocality in any single text. Even in "Recitatif," a first-person narrative, the narrator is undercut by her own contradictory and partial information. But Morrison develops a clear and insistent authorial voice that speaks through a variety of narrators. Her inimitable power inheres in this ability to seamlessly interweave form, content, and meaning in a deceptively facile manner.

Raymond Hedin has noted that the "coherence of Morrison's vision" is inherent in the structure that "parses out its logic into repeating patterns that offer the reader no solace or refuge from [her] anger."[20] Yet Morrison's ordered, organically structured anger is thematized in form and character. Consider her use of names and behavior to register her hostility toward certain characters—women whose names end with the graphemes -*ine*, -*ene*, and -*een*: Geraldine, Jadine, Pauline, Helene, and Maureen. The behavior of the women who bear such names provides clues to Morrison's attitude toward them. Maureen is a young girl obsessed with her fair complexion that sets her apart from the darker children in the community; Helene is impatient with black people who do not recognize her as the exemplar of decorum; Pauline is so preoccupied with the "rightness" of whiteness that she does not care what happens to her dark-skinned child; and Jadine is conflicted by both her success in the white world and her connection to the black world, Africa included. The names given these characters represent one method by which Morrison encodes her displeasure with certain characters and nudges her reader toward a collusion.

Commenting on the African American "artistic presence," Morrison states, "We are the subjects of our own narrative, witnesses to and participants in our own experience, and, in no way coincidentally, in the experience of those with whom we have come in contact. We are not . . . 'other' . . . and to read imaginative literature by and about us is to choose to examine centers of the self and to have the opportunity to compare these centers with the 'raceless' one with which we are, all of us, most familiar" ("Unspeakable Things" 9). To this end, Morrison's fiction mirrors her search for metaphorical forms that assist African Americans in recovering their lost or diminished selves. These narratives present several characters—marginalized figures within an already marginal community—seeking to carve a space for themselves within the chronicles of their communities. Morrison is also concerned with *how* things happened because, as she puts it, "why is difficult to handle" (*Bluest Eye* 9). She has stated that, since "memories and recollections" cannot give her complete access to the "unwritten internal life" of her ancestors, she must rely on "imagination" to give her a roundabout access. Limited access notwithstanding, she must remain faithful to the world of her ancestors: "Infidelity to that milieu—the absence of the interior life, the deliberate excising of it from the records that the slaves themselves told—is precisely the problem in the discourse that proceeded without us" ("Unspeakable Things" 9). That discourse is, of course, the discourse of the master narrative, the view from white observers and white writers, whose voices often were presumed to be the authentic voices on black life in the United States.

Hortense J. Spillers has articulated a need for this strategic reading of texts by African American women writers by urging a critique of these women's work "in their total and dynamic historical situatedness"; by which she means that critical practice should not be restricted to traditional notions of African American literature that center on issues of race and class alone ("Cross-Currents" 258).[21] Although the question of race cannot be ignored in African American fiction, it should not dwarf other ways of reading it. Spillers persuasively argues that, while we may be on the cusp of the "post-race subject," it would be foolish to ignore the reality of race. Spillers further notes that Morrison's fiction demands a "widened critical awareness" without a renunciation of "its inexorable ties" to the African American struggle for equality in all its dimensions ("All the Things" 137).

Morrison avers that African Americans must share a great deal of the blame for this cultural loss that often results from self-betrayal.[22] Her fiction suggests that to overcome psychological violence African Americans must regain their cultural integrity, which is most effectively accomplished through communal efforts that recognize and respect individual differences. Morrison's fiction especially calls attention to the power of language to construct alternative ways of viewing the African American experience. Speaking of the role of the African American tradition in her work, Morrison underscores her aesthetic project: "If my work is faithfully to reflect the aesthetic tradition of Afro-American culture, it must make conscious use of the characteristics of its art forms and translate them into print: antiphony, the group nature of art, its functionality, its improvisational nature, its relationship to audience performance, the critical voice which upholds tradition and communal values and which also provides occasion for an individual to transcend and/or defy group restrictions" ("Memory" 388–89).

I have framed analyses around Morrison's representations of difference. I examine instances where individuals are unfairly scrutinized and unjustly ostracized, even mocked, because their bodies are different from those around them. I also look briefly at certain characters who view their bodies as superior to those of their neighbors based on the degree of melanin in their skin. Such characters as Maureen, Geraldine, and Jadine have been read along color lines, while Sula, Eva, and Pilate have been read as bodies with distinct markers or missing body parts.[23] Maggie, Beloved, and the 8-rocks can be read in the context of the politics of difference—how they view their bodies and how their bodies are viewed by others—signifying both power and powerlessness.

A brief look at Pilate may serve as one example of reading such bodies. Pilate's absent navel—the mark of (dis)connection—renders her so different that the community "felt pity along with their terror of having been in the company of something God never made" (*Song* 144). The absence of this maternal link situates Pilate in a space that cannot accommodate her. Through Pilate, Morrison complicates notions of identity based on factors other than race and reveals that within the African American community blacks themselves may lack the power or position to be called "racists," but they are, nevertheless, capable and guilty of egregious prejudices. In *The Bluest Eye* the young children circling Pecola refer to her as "black e mo [black even more than they are], yadaddsleepsnekked," to which Claudia muses,

> They had extemporized a verse made up of two insults about matters over which the victim had no control: the color of her skin and speculations on the sleeping habits of an adult, wildly fitting in its incoherence. That they themselves were black . . . was irrelevant. It was their contempt for their own blackness that gave the first insult its teeth. They seemed to have taken their exquisitely learned self-hatred, their elaborately designed hopelessness, and sucked it all up into a fiery cone of scorn that had burned for ages in the hollows of their minds. (55)

Morrison's simultaneous indictment of white racism and black prejudice in this passage speaks directly to the concerns of this study, the ways in which Morrison *plays with*, stages, and critiques these issues in her fiction. The circling children mirror Morrison's narrative gesture of leading the reader around the subject of racism and verbal abuse. Morrison, like the community, allows us to see the many points from which Pecola is damaged. The "ugliness" heaped on Pecola exposes the reader to the ugliness that engages Morrison as a writer.

Morrison explodes myths about difference by refiguring aesthetics in what has traditionally been deemed ugly, unnatural, freakish—all the negative baggage we bring to physical differences. It must be noted, however, that such notions of difference are generally measured against some standard of normativity—color, phenotypic features, presence or absence and arrangement of certain body parts. Morrison does not pretend *not* to see such differences. In her fiction, the discourse surrounding the physically handicapped, those with maimed and warped bodies, is often direct and blunt. Through such directness Morrison forces us to look directly at those individuals—even those we find visually repulsive—and avoid euphemisms. One such direct, in-your-face discourse is expressed by the people in the Bottom who "knew Shadrack was *crazy* but that did not mean that he didn't have any sense or, even more important, that he had no power" (*Sula* 15; emphasis added). Through such gestures Morrison is able simultaneously to sign difference and to destabilize our notions about difference. What appears on the surface may not represent the whole person.

2 *Playing with Difference: The Other as Subject*

> If I had to live in a racial house, it was important, at the least, to rebuild it so that it was not a windowless prison into which I was forced, a thick-walled, impenetrable container from which no cry could be heard, but rather an open house, grounded, yet generous in its supply of windows and doors. Or, at the most, it became imperative for me to transform this house completely. Counterracism was never an option.
>
> —Toni Morrison, "Home"

For enslaved Africans, race was destiny; race determined the places they and their posterity would occupy in this nation. Race was and continues to be a physical and a mental space: places set aside on the nation's physical terrain and within the black psyche, a constant reminder to African Americans of their difference and otherness.

For Morrison, the problematics of being a raced writer and a raced subject raise certain fundamental questions: "How to be both free and situated: how to convert a racist house into a race-specific yet nonracist home. How to enunciate race while depriving it of its lethal cling" ("Home" 5). Such questions pose for Morrison "aesthetic" and "political" choices. She has stated that as a writer she must decide how to shape African American experiences within an imaginary space that gives not just expression but credibility to those experiences. She has also stated that she must decide what aspects of her own life as a black woman, intimately knowledgeable about the black experience, provide the best examples of African American life. In short, if she intends to be faithful to her ethnic community and to the integrity of her art, she must embrace both her racialized self and her racial community. For Morrison, these are not competing but inextricable and mutually nurturing positions.

At the core of Morrison's fiction is the issue of how to construct race as a discursive subject and simultaneously create individual subjectivities and the possibilities for intersubjective relations. Jessica Benjamin has observed that to achieve intersubjectivity the "other must be recognized as another subject in order for the self to fully experience his or her subjectivity in another's presence" (30). Achieving intersubjective relations, however, is often difficult because of real and perceived barriers. Such barriers include physical manifestations of difference such as "racial" features. When Morrison asserts that once race enters her texts, even as she attempts to reduce its relevance or situate it at the margins while foregrounding different categories of identity, she is, nevertheless, aware that race is such a powerful image that it is certain to mobilize expectations. As she has pointed out, although race is only one mark of observable difference, the term itself is layered with many preconceptions and prejudices. Graham Richards articulates the problem: "The heart of the difficulty is that we are still operating in a cultural context where racialized discourse is inescapable, while simultaneously trying to transcend this. Our linguistic differences therefore signify both the contradictions inherent in this situation and the problems we face in trying to resolve it" (xvii). Fiction, in its attempts to replicate and represent human experiences, offers some possibilities for resolving the dilemma posed by racialized discourse.

Race, to cite Henry Louis Gates Jr., affords us opportunities for scrutinizing the "ways in which writing relates to race, how attitudes toward racial differences generate and structure literary texts by us *and* about us." We must, however, as Gates observes, accept the fact that race is now both a "persistent" and "implicit presence" ("Writing" 15).[1] Morrison herself speaks about the inescapability of race as a category of literary critique because race is embedded in most American literature ("Race and Literature"). While biologists and anthropologists argue that within the human community there is no such category as race, the term itself, as well as its referents, still seems to engage scholars as a useful rubric for identifying various groups within the human family. Kwame Anthony Appiah has noted this contradiction between what is perceived as a "real" category of identity and what is defined as a cultural construction: "It comes as a shock to many to learn that there is fairly wide-spread consensus in the sciences of biology and anthropology that the word 'race,' at least as it is used in most unscientific discussions, refers to nothing that science should recognize as real." Moreover, Appiah continues, "races are like witches: however unreal witches are, *belief* in witches, like belief in races, has had—and in many communities continues to have—profound consequences for human social life" ("Race" 277).[2]

In her desire to reveal some ways in which race occupies a central position within American society, Morrison has created racialized subjects who are indeed conscious of their positions. Her use of race as a trope of difference and marginalization speaks to the pervasiveness of race matters in the United States as a systemic and recurring issue that frequently determines the social, economic, and gendered relationships within and across class and ethnic borders (see West, *Race Matters*). As Gates puts it, "The sense of difference defined in popular usages of the term 'race' has both described and *inscribed* differences of language, belief system, artistic tradition, . . . rhythm, athletic ability, cerebration" ("Writing" 5).[3] It is evident from such race theories and from narratives about race that, as a social and cultural construction, race can be deconstructed, even dismantled. This is, then, one of Morrison's major strategies: to craft race narratives and artfully deconstruct them. To begin this investigation of Morrison's construction and deconstruction of difference, I want to turn to three of her fictional texts: "Recitatif," *Beloved,* and *Tar Baby.*

"Recitatif" uses female subjects to elide and sort out a number of ideological and narrative issues based around difference. As a narrative of seeming indeterminacy, "Recitatif," with its first-person narrator, serves Morrison's purpose most effectively as a layered construction with multiple meanings. In its concern with identity politics, this short story is self-reflexive. It deliberately foregrounds, obfuscates, and collapses difference. The narrative sets up expectations and then topples them by showing us how much we rely on limited and stereotypical information in order to draw conclusions about certain characters and certain events. The narrative also exposes our tendency at times to equate race and class. Even when race is not specified and class is, we sometimes assign individuals to a given race based solely on information about their class. It is the uncertainty about the relationship of race to class and about other aspects of difference at the level of plot and exposition that propels some readers toward assumptions about racial identities. When Twyla, the narrator in "Recitatif," gives certain details and withholds others, readers' racial interpretations may be forestalled or severely tested. Twyla's uncertainty about and insistence on Maggie's (the maid's) racial identity introduce the issue of racialized subjects, class, and physical differences. Even so, race is not the overriding issue in this narrative, but it does become the preoccupation of some readers.

For certain readers, the text's clearly charted warnings may not be enough. Elizabeth Abel, for instance, admits to a frustration in trying to sort out who is black and who is white in "Recitatif" and concedes that the text "forc[es] us to construct racial categories from highly ambiguous social cues." Abel also recognizes Morrison's strategy of deliberately positing ambiguities by noting that Morrison inserts Maggie into the narrative as "a figure of racial undecidability" ("Black Writing" 472). In contradistinction to the other characters, Maggie is the only one whose physical features we know with certainty, that is, if we accept Twyla's descriptions of her. Maggie's legs are described as "parentheses" (245); she is a deaf-mute. She represents a physical difference that, unlike color and race, is not culturally constructed but does have profound cultural implications in terms of how she is treated by others. Only in terms of race, as with Twyla and Roberta, is Maggie a figure of undecidability. Other aspects of her identity emerge: she is a maid (a sign of her economic and social status); she is physically deformed; she is an older woman, a mute, who cannot speak when she is taunted and assaulted by Twyla and Roberta and the older girls at St. Bonaventure Orphanage. These identifiable characteristics render Maggie a metonymic figure for those stigmatized and cruelly treated because of their physical differences. Maggie is decidedly the figure on which the narrative turns. Through her the text strongly suggests that we often look at other people's bodies and conclude that, because their bodies are different from the so-called norm, they are somehow flawed and are, therefore, less human. Significantly, Twyla and Roberta are never certain about Maggie's race. They remember her more pronounced physical features, which signify to them their right to verbally abuse her: "Dummy! Dummy!" "Bow legs!" (245). Although Twyla is remorseful about their behavior toward Maggie and expresses sympathy that "there was somebody in there [inside the deformed body] after all who heard us call her those names and couldn't tell us" (245), the question of whether that "somebody" was black or white is never settled because Maggie's race is not the issue, however much Twyla and Roberta try to make it an issue. Maggie's physical attributes are flashpoints of the narrative. Through Twyla's observation about Maggie's humanity, the narrative suggests that behind the exterior physical markers—the color of one's skin, the shape of one's body, the absence of one's ability to speak—is a human subject, which may be masked by viewers'/readers' focus on such surface markers.

Maggie has another function in the narrative that relates directly to Twyla and Roberta's treatment of her and their inability to forget her long after they have left the orphanage. Maggie represents Twyla's and Roberta's projected anger and resentment at their mothers' neglect and abandonment. Looking, perhaps, for some adult figure to attack for their loss of maternal attention, the girls find Maggie an easy target.[4] Maggie's muteness represents their mothers' failure to meet their emotional needs. Twyla's description of Maggie as a midget—"She wasn't much taller than we were . . . dressing like a kid and never saying anything at all" (245)—suggests an unconscious but oblique description of her own mother, who, according to Twyla, dresses and behaves "like she was the little girl looking for her mother—not me" (246). More revealing, however, is Twyla's response to her mother's show of affection—"Twyla, baby. Twyla, baby!"—which at first embarrasses Twyla and then pleases her: "I couldn't stay mad at Mary. . . . I wanted to stay buried in her fur all day." This moment of maternal affection causes Twyla to briefly forget about Roberta and even forgive her own mother for her outrageous dress and conduct, because, Twyla concedes, "a pretty mother on earth is better than a beautiful dead one in the sky even if she did leave you all alone to go dancing" (247).

"My mother danced all night and Roberta's was sick" (243), Twyla tells us, suggesting present but absent parents—each parent self-absorbed and preoccupied with her personal concerns, dancing and illness respectively. The girls' constant references to Maggie, often in juxtaposition to their conversations about their mothers, suggest that Maggie is more than a figure of difference: metaphorically, she is a warped mother figure who fails to respond to Twyla's and Roberta's needs to be nurtured. Her little "kid's hat with ear flaps" (245) at once signifies her closing her ears to whatever insults the girls hurl at her and, coextensively, their mothers' preoccupation with themselves at the expense of their daughters' needs. Consider Twyla's question to Roberta at a subsequent meeting: "Remember Maggie? The day she fell down and those gar girls laughed at her?" Roberta counters, "No, Twyla. They knocked her down. Those girls pushed her down and tore her clothes. . . . You've blocked it, Twyla. It happened." To quell her discomfort about and her complicity in the mistreatment of Maggie, Twyla changes the subject, but "the Maggie thing was troubling [her]" (254). Their final conversation and the last words in the story are about their mothers and Maggie: the admission on both sides that their mothers never changed nor did their desire to know what became of Maggie. Twyla and Roberta rather casually dismiss their mothers, who are where they were when the girls first met—dancing and ill. Their ongoing concern, however, can be read as regret for both their unkindness to and their loss of Maggie, the displaced mother figure. Their conversations, centered around Maggie, direct the reader toward a maternal discourse and the narrative's focus on its own project—away from the problem of racial identity and toward the issue of child neglect and mother-daughter relations.

Nearly twenty-five years after their stay at the orphanage, Roberta remarks to Twyla, "I really did think [Maggie] was black. . . . But now I can't be sure. I just remember her as old, so old. And because she couldn't talk—well, you know, I thought she was crazy" (261). Roberta's very revealing dismissal of Maggie's race and physical deformities leads her to denigrate Maggie's mind. Her description of Maggie is as cruel and as totalizing as Twyla's mother's conclusion about all people of Roberta's race. Through the distinguishing features and details about these characters' behavior, Morrison throws into question a system of difference that demands serious considerations about how we come to judge individuals on the basis of observable features. In Roberta's brief statement about Maggie, Morrison harnesses an array of prejudices directed toward the elderly, the disabled, and those perceived to be black.

But readers such as Abel are not necessarily satisfied with this seemingly inadequate narrative closure. To satisfy her desire for racial specificity, Abel, citing the parallel reading of African American critic Lula Fragd and others, constructs an analysis of the text along a cultural axis by noting Roberta's interest in the African American guitarist Jimi Hendrix, whose name offers no concrete proof that Roberta is black or white, even though she is headed to his concert and Twyla has never heard of Jimi Hendrix. In terms of Morrison's strategy it is important to note that most of the attendees at Hendrix's concerts were whites. Unable to pinpoint racially identifiable bodies among the three women representing aspects of difference in "Recitatif," Abel, submitting to the intentional fallacy,[5] decided to approach Morrison directly but gained no more from the author than a suggestion to look for her answers not in racial codes but in class distinctions. Abel, clearly disappointed in Morrison's reply, admits that Morrison raised more questions by stating that "her project in this story was to substitute class for racial codes in order to drive a wedge between these typically elided categories" ("Black Writing" 476). It is at the point of Morrison's refusal to give Abel a definitive answer that we may begin an alternative reading of "Recitatif." It is important to note, however, that sometimes readers' preoccupation with what is concealed may blind them to what is overtly expressed.

In "Recitatif" readers are confronted with a set of deliberate ambiguities about race and its relevance to unfolding events. This narrative confounds both characters and readers to the extent that what they think they know about race turns out to be an epistemological exercise in indeterminacy. Because the notion of identity is so confounded, readers must constantly rethink received notions of difference based on race and class and question their own investment in the cultural constructions of such categories. The narrative discourse may force some readers to reach for stereotypes and presumptions about race in order to sort out identities. Furthermore, the narrative complicates reliance upon racial differences by suggesting that difference is sometimes an unreliable marker that may expose some deeply held notions about identity. Readers are sometimes trapped by false clues. As readers we may devote too much attention to minor signs and markers and spend too little time sorting out the numerous ways by which the construction of this narrative brings readers into the narrative *process*. More important is Morrison's ability to expose the racial biases readers sometimes bring to certain texts, even when those texts do not stress race.

In "Recitatif," race itself, or any direct reference to it, is used only sparingly, yet the story plays on readers' desire to know and to positively identify the characters by race. In order to achieve this desired outcome, Morrison, in avoiding racial identifications, states that she made a conscious decision "to be forced as a writer not to be lazy and rely on obvious codes"; she, then, had to discuss each character "in a complicated way—as a person" (Schappell 102). Morrison's strategy is evident when Twyla identifies herself and the other female protagonist by names— Twyla Johnson and Roberta Fisk—and refers to Roberta as a "girl from a whole other race" (243), which she never specifies. The embedded narrative about Maggie mirrors the outer narrative in its refusal to be race-specific. The text frustrates those readers who desire racial specificity by calling attention to the girls' behavior toward Maggie, who represents physical deformity, not racial difference, since she is no more clear to the girls in terms of race than the girls' racial identities are to readers. This strategy suggests that race matters to us even though the story takes race for granted and moves on to those specific ways in which race should not and does *not* matter. The structure of "Recitatif" opens the possibility that readers are sometimes more vested in the attribution of race to individual characters than they are in the underlying issues that unite and separate the characters. What is problematic for some readers—which girl

is black and which is white—poses no problem for Twyla or Roberta after their initial meeting.

By hoisting certain flags—terms like "whole other race," "salt and
pepper," "sandy-colored"—the text exploits the racial baggage readers
sometimes bring to a text. Twyla and Roberta share memories of a few
months of bonding through similar backgrounds and several years of divergent and intersecting paths, engendering conflicts that are not so easily resolved as those conflicts present during their first meeting at the
orphanage. The narrative traces the girls' friendship from their lives together as eight-year-olds in an orphanage through two subsequent meet-
ings, spaced over twenty years. Although these girls are from different
races, they share equivalent parental neglect. Twyla readily assumes that
the information her mother has given her about the "other race" is true:
"They never washed their hair and they smelled funny" (243). Only once
in the course of the narrative does Twyla mention any confirmation of
this "important" information from her mother—that Roberta did "smell
funny." It is, in fact, Twyla's mother who teaches her daughter about the
other group's "smell" and about the differences separating the races. Twyla
describes Roberta's smell as "funny," which can be read as just "different from" Twyla's "smell" and not from some noisome sign of race. Again,
Twyla reveals her mother's predisposing her to racist attitudes when she
and Roberta are introduced to each other as roommates: "My mother
won't like you putting me in here" (243), she tells Mrs. Itkin, the director of the orphanage, who—indicating no understanding of or desire to
know why Twyla's mother would object to her being placed in a room with
Roberta—quips, "Good. . . . Maybe then she'll come and take you home."
Failing in her efforts to get what is presumed a favorable and compliant
response, Twyla asks the implied reader, "How's that for mean?" (243). It
is evident from the movement of the opening scenario that Twyla is testing and seeking confirmation of her mother's theories about the other race.

Twyla admits that she and Roberta "didn't like each other all that
much at first." However, once they become better acquainted and attend
the same classes, their racial differences ("we looked like salt and pepper
standing there" [244]) become less significant to their friendship. Twyla
subsequently admits that she "liked the way [Roberta] understood things
so fast" (244). Collusive and inclusive language—"we" and "us" ("We got
along all right, Roberta and me")—signals their bonding. Now they share
more than just a room; they share similar academic standing in three
classes—"F's in civics and communication skills and gym" (245)—and
equivalent status as "dumped" state children. Their status as "dumped"
rather than "real orphans" with "beautiful dead parents in the sky" en-

genders prejudice based not on their racial differences but on their common status as neglected children. According to Twyla, "Even the New York City Puerto Ricans and the upstate Indians ignored us" (244). The insertion of two other minorities undercuts notions of racial or cultural solidarity within the orphanage and reinforces class distinctions—girls of dead parents are considered better than those with living parents like Twyla's and Roberta's. Additionally, the other orphans' indifference reinforces Morrison's project of deflecting attention from the girls' racial identities.

Although race does not determine Twyla's and Roberta's identities, race seems a greater concern and an effective divider for their mothers. Roberta's attempt to introduce the two mothers is unsuccessful. When Twyla's mother—who has already prejudiced her daughter against the "other race"—extends her hand to Roberta's mother, the latter turns away. And while Twyla's mother is the one who has taught her daughter that the "other" race smells funny, that she wouldn't like sharing a room with that "other," it is Roberta's mother who manifests her aversion to Twyla's mother. On one level readers may understand this aversion as a racial one; however, the detailed account of other aspects separating the mothers complicates this scenario. Twyla's mother wears tight green pants and a "fur jacket with the pocket linings so ripped she had to pull to get her hands out of them" (246). Twyla's emotional response when she sees her after a twenty-eight-day separation is initially not the joy of reunion but a resentment toward her mother's attire. Roberta's mother is a decided contrast to Twyla's, not because the two women are from different races but because of Mrs. Johnson's pious facade—her ponderous cross-shaped pendant, "like two telephone poles" (253), and the "biggest Bible ever made" (247). Is it race, class, or socioreligious differences signaled by their attires? Such details shift our focus from their physical features to their physical trappings.

Twyla's mother has also told her daughter that people of the other race never wash themselves. Yet the image of Roberta's mother is that of a well-scrubbed and polished pharisee. The mothers themselves feel different, but the difference is equivocal. Twyla's mother tries to inculcate an awareness of racial differences in her daughter through stereotypes, while Roberta's mother actualizes what appears to be racism—her refusal to shake hands with or even acknowledge Twyla's mother. Mrs. Fisk's slight to Mrs. Johnson may be her invitation to readers, like Twyla's earlier aside, to censure Mrs. Johnson's attire. Yet both mothers behave hypocritically: Twyla's mother, in her gesture of courtesy that belies what she has taught her daughter; and Roberta's mother—despite her conspicuous display of a Christian symbol—in her rebuff of Twyla's mother that exhibits a superficial adherence to Christian practices. Subsequently, Twyla's assessment of her friendship with Roberta when they were young, isolated, neglected girls in an orphanage makes it clear that their early conditioning about race has been ineffectual: "Those four months were nothing in time. Maybe it was the thing itself. Just being there, together. Two little girls who knew what nobody else in the world knew—how not to ask questions. How to believe what had to be believed. There was politeness in that reluctance and generosity as well. Is your mother sick too? No, she dances all night. Oh—and an understanding nod" (253).

Twyla's rehearsal of their relationship at St. Bonaventure comes belatedly—some twenty years after the fact and at an age when she can look back with a mature gaze. Her assessment of their earlier friendship includes their meeting at Howard Johnson's. "Once, twelve years ago," Twyla muses, "we passed like strangers. A black girl and a white girl meeting in a Howard Johnson's on a road and having nothing to say. . . . Now we were behaving like sisters separated for much too long" (253). It must be noted, however, that when Twyla and Roberta first meet after they leave the orphanage they are as distant as their mothers were some twelve years earlier: the distance is similarly ambiguous, but based on cultural knowledge and social sophistication. When Twyla steps up to greet Roberta at a Howard Johnson's restaurant, she gets a cold reception. Twyla immediately feels the chasm between them—not a racial separation but a social one, partly marked by the contrast between Twyla's Howard Johnson's uniform and Roberta's "powder-blue halter and shorts outfit and earrings the size of bracelets" (249); "One in a blue and white triangle waitress hat—the other on her way to see Hendrix" (253). But there is nothing overtly racial about their contrasting positions. Moreover, most servers in Howard Johnson restaurants in the early 1970s were white.

Several years after their Howard Johnson meeting, class again separates them. They meet in a grocery store specializing in foods for gourmets, a place where Roberta purchases food for her family and where Twyla goes in "just to see" or to select items that "would sit in [her] cupboard for years." Roberta, on the other hand, purchases "a bunch of asparagus and two cartons of fancy water" with the same panache she shows in wearing "diamonds . . . and [a] smart white summer dress" (251). To Twyla, Roberta's marriage to a wealthy man from the "IBM crowd" contrasts sharply with her marriage to a fireman. Roberta—with a "dark blue limousine" and "Chinaman" chauffeur—is an oppositional figure to Twyla, whose purse is laden with coupons. When Twyla privately muses that she "was dying to know what happened to [Roberta], how she got from Jimi Hendrix to Annandale, a neighborhood full of doctors and IBM executives," and that "everything is easy for them" (252), it is not at all clear who "they" are. Are "they" upwardly mobile blacks and/or whites? The socially adept? Or are "they" the "smart IBM people" or the "rich IBM people"? Newburgh does not provide clues to Twyla's and Roberta's race; we know only that the town is populated by people on welfare and by people from middle and upper classes (250–51). These features of the narrative register class differences, not racial divides.

Later, when Twyla and Roberta are divided over the bussing issue, they never mention race. In fact, Twyla describes the bussing crisis as a sign of the divided community. In framing the face-off between Twyla and Roberta over the bussing issue, the narrative further complicates their racial identities ("Strife came to us that fall. . . . Racial strife," as the newspapers depicted it [255]) by having the two women carry picket signs that—while reinforcing their individual positions—say nothing about their race. The text frames the terms of difference as a battle over the rights of mothers and children. Roberta's sign reads, "MOTHERS HAVE RIGHTS TOO!" (256)—the right to decide where their children will go to school? Twyla's sign counters and reinforces Roberta's: "AND SO DO CHIL-DREN*** . . . Have rights" (258). What rights? To attend a good school? The issues of who is bussed and to where may speak to both race and class issues, but the racial identity question is not conclusively answered. The absence of discourse that reduces characters to simplistic or generalized racial subjects limits the potential for reducing them to one-dimensional subjects. Rather, Morrison acknowledges the interplay of a number of human elements—early socialization, personality, class, and social sophistication. In this short story, Morrison exposes ambiguity and the diversity of interpretation.

Morrison has spoken elsewhere about the centrality of playing with race in "Recitatif": "I withheld information about race for a couple of reasons. One principal reason was I wanted to sort of underscore how we distort race, how we have so much baggage ourselves as readers that we bring to a narrative. . . . If you say they're black, then they're black. If you don't identify race, the assumption is that . . . they're white." Morrison continues, "It doesn't mean that race doesn't matter. It matters a great deal, but that's because we've made it matter. . . . But, when you think about one-on-one relationships, it doesn't" (Rose 3). In "Recitatif" race is less important to Twyla and Roberta's relationship at the orphanage because their loneliness and need for companionship overshadow their racial differences. Morrison confided to Charlie Rose that she derives pleasure, arguably at readers' expense, from withholding specific racial information about Twyla and Roberta "because I know why they [readers] think that one is white" (Rose 3). Morrison has also spoken of "the pleasure [she] took and still [takes] in being able to withhold racial markers" and the "enormous leap" it meant for her in terms of her giving readers "every thing about [the characters] except one small thing . . . race" ("Race and Literature").

For readers in search of raced bodies, it may not be difficult to leap from race to racism. The desire for differentiated differences, differences within difference, is a need for manifest differences and marked bodies. Once bodies are identified, it may seem easier to know whom to accept and whom to reject. Since Twyla is specific about her and Roberta's relationships over time, why do we not accept their behavior with all its implications of difference and formulate our judgments about them within the constructs of the text's clever delineation? Is it because we are not satisfied or even comfortable with representations of these highly vexed issues? Is it because we need characters like Maggie, whose body we can read? Is it only then that we can know who is one of "us" or one of "them"? "Recitatif" compels readers to question assumptions about difference and may even lead them to discover repressed or latent biases. In constructing a self-reflexive and reader-centered narrative, Morrison adroitly leads us to the principal subject of "Recitatif"—the reader.

In *Beloved*, as in "Recitatif," Morrison embeds a narrative about two women differentiated primarily by race, but whose backgrounds and immediate situation bring them together in a space that diminishes the importance of their racial difference. And in *Beloved*, as in "Recitatif," the issue of racial difference is dealt with at the beginning of the encounter and then recedes—as Sethe and Amy's immediate situation calls for mutual dependency—only to resurface at the end of their shared experience. In one sense, they are both orphaned by the political and economic systems from which they are fleeing. But, unlike Roberta and Twyla, Amy and Sethe do have "beautiful dead parents in the sky." That is not what brings them to the woods near the Ohio River; they are fugitives from systems of indenture and slavery respectively. However, once they breach the boundaries of racial conditioning, race *seems* to be inconsequential; yet, all the while, race lurks at the margins, ready to assert itself when, and if, actions by one or both of the women thrust them into differentiated psychosocial and political spaces in what for each means intimacy and "home" (as discussed in Martin and Mohanty). Twyla and Roberta and Amy and Sethe find themselves in such contradictory spaces.

Sethe and Amy's meeting commands our attention in a different way. In *Beloved,* a narrative about the cooperative meeting between a black woman and a white woman, Morrison presents us with another view of difference based on gender and class matters that do not implicate us so much as readers by exposing our racial attitudes. Rather, the text lays out the racial and class dynamics between Amy and Sethe and allows us to interpret these dynamics as momentary hurdles, soon diminished by the conjunction of gender and need, played out in a sphere where both race and class lose their significance.

Amy and Sethe represent an era and an ethos that would—given the norms of that society—complicate their meeting.[6] However, Morrison is able to dissolve the "customary configurations of this liminality"—"silence, subjection, humiliation, submissiveness, acceptance of pain"—by transforming these stereotypes into figural constructs, thereby offering her readers an emotional experience of the power women can derive from "structural transcendence" (Mascia-Lees 106). At the moment of their meeting, Amy calls attention to Sethe's race—"Look there. A nigger" (32)—and alerts readers to Sethe's pregnancy. Amy's rudeness is expressed in the liberty she takes in asking Sethe, "Whose baby that?" (78). But Sethe's situation—her fugitive status, her race, and her pregnancy (despite her threat to "eat" the person who posed a barrier to her successful escape)—demands that she behave cautiously. So while Amy insults her, Sethe reserves her thoughts, which are revealed to Denver years later and are no less charitable than Amy's: "'I was hungry,' she told Denver, 'just as hungry as I could be for his eyes [thinking the voice to be a male's]. I couldn't wait.' . . . 'Come here,' I was thinking. 'Be the last thing you behold.'" Instead of a male Sethe sees "the raggediest-looking trash you ever saw saying, 'Look there. A nigger. If that don't beat all'" (31–32). When we juxtapose the terms "nigger" and "trash," we discover the similarity in the women's racist discourse. Yet the potentially divisive language is mentally set aside by Sethe, whose immediate response to Amy's insults is reserved for Denver's telling: "Then she did the magic: lifted Sethe's feet and legs and massaged them until she cried salt tears" (35). Morrison allows Denver's version of Amy and Sethe's meeting to carry the weight of Sethe's emotions in order to reveal Denver's loneliness and interior world and to indicate Sethe's awareness that it was politic, while she was dependent upon Amy, to say as little as necessary. It is clear from both Sethe's and Amy's initial responses to each other that they are speaking and thinking from habit and conditioning, not necessarily from conviction. The insertion of a white woman in the scene of Sethe's escape from slavery accounts for what Mascia-Lees terms "double liminality"

(106). Sethe and Amy's encounter engages the discourse of bondage and racism that separates the two women and the acts of freedom and compassion that unite them. The text elaborates Sethe's and Amy's disparate spheres of bondage and their shared site of bonding by showing how difference and commonality emerge out of the overt racism and classism in their brief encounter. Their encounter along the Ohio River demonstrates that race is not always an effective divider and that habits of being are often undermined by need.

In addition to their closeness in ages (Amy is a year younger than Sethe), Sethe and Amy share romantic sensibilities and brilliant imaginations. Amy loves the sun—though she has had only two opportunities to really savor it: "Sleeping with the sun in your face is the best old feeling. . . . Two times I did it. Once when I was little. . . . Next time, in back of the wagon, it happened" (80). Amy's very journey attests to this romantic spirit: she's off to Boston to find velvet, which for her is "like the world was just born. Clean and new and so smooth" (33). She sings for Sethe during their night in the woods. Gently, she traces the wounds on Sethe's back in one of the most poignant enunciations of the brutal effects of slavery: "It's a tree. . . . A chokecherry tree. See, here's the trunk—it's red and split wide open, full of sap, and this here's the parting for the branches. . . . Leaves, too, look like, and dern if these ain't blossoms. Tiny little cherry blossoms, just as white. Your back got a whole tree on it. In bloom. What God have in mind, I wonder" (79). Through Amy's initial musing on Sethe's wounds, Sethe has an opportunity to "see" through Amy's description just how badly she has been beaten. The treelike scarification heals, but the configuration remains. And while Sethe cannot see the mark, it has been seared into her memory and has become for her a symbol of slavery and the impetus for her flight. As she later tells Paul D, "I got a tree on my back. . . . I've never seen it and never will. But that's what [Amy] said it looked like. . . . A chokecherry tree" (15–16). When Paul D sees the "tree," he, like Amy, is moved to a poignant eloquence in the face of the horror the wound invokes.[7] He "saw the sculpture her back had become, like the decorative work of an ironsmith too passionate for display" (17). Like Amy, Paul D traces the contours of Sethe's wounded back, "none of which Sethe could feel because her back skin had been dead for years" (18). The "tree" is a "hieroglyphics of the flesh"[8]—a visual and tactile narrative of Sethe's personal suffering and the strength of her resolve—that ramifies to embrace the whole history of African American suffering. This configuration of the "chokecherry" tree is a trope for the African American "family tree" of wounds dating from the slave trade. Her play on the word "chokecherry" directs readers toward the trees used for hanging blacks during the Ku Klux Klan's reign of terror during and after Reconstruction. Victims of such hangings were referred to in songs and stories as "strange fruit,"[9] a metaphor for the black bodies strung from trees and often witnessed by crowds in a carnivalesque atmosphere. Stamp Paid refers to "eighty-seven lynchings in one year alone in Kentucky," "necks broken," as he fingers a "red ribbon knotted around a curl of wet woolly hair, clinging still to its bit of scalp." "What *are* these people?" he asks in horror (180). Through these characters' meditations on the brutality of slavery, readers are directed toward the intricate construction of language and meaning, toward the interplay of sign and signification. To read Sethe's wounds is to read history through the eyes of those who witnessed it. Readers become part of this history by virtue of their responsibility for filling in the literal spaces glossed by Amy's and Paul D's metaphorical accounts.

Like Amy, Sethe is a romantic, despite her enslavement. She brings flowers and herbs into the Garner household "just to be able to work in it, to feel like some part of it was hers" (22). In the young Sethe we see the inchoate insurgency that later demands maternal autonomy, which the slave system has denied her. Years later Sethe mocks this drive toward a personal aesthetic: "As though a handful of myrtle stuck in the handle of a pressing iron propped against the door in a whitewoman's kitchen could make it hers. As though mint sprig in the mouth changed the breath as well as its odor. A bigger fool never lived" (23–24). But this admission of her foolishness does not prevent Sethe, at age fourteen, from making her marriage more ceremonious than the typical slave marriage. Sethe's actions as a young slave girl are insurgent acts against the inhumaneness of slavery because, as she tells Beloved, "I didn't want it to be me just moving over a bit of pallet full of corn husks. Or just me bringing my night bucket into his cabin" (58). For her wedding ceremony Sethe makes what she terms a "bedding dress" from fragments of disparate items belonging to her mistress, Lillian Garner. The result is a quilted garment that weaves together mementos from the kind Lillian Garner and symbols of Sethe's life and work at the Garner farm. More importantly, however, the garment reveals Sethe's humanity and resistance to attempts at denying her a "traditional" woman's rite of passage. Sethe's memory of her wedding contains the seeds of her emergent resistance to domination and oppression.

When Sethe and Amy speak of moments of natural beauty and their own creative gestures, we learn about aspects of their lives that could not be contained nor constrained within their respective systems of bondage. Their imaginations find free play within the constraints of their respec-

tive environments. The surreptitious methods they use to vent their romantic spirits place them among the Morrisonian characters—Sula and
Pauline, for example—who are described as "artist[s] with no art form"
(*Sula* 121)[10] or lacking "paints and crayons" (*Bluest* 89). Moreover, in the
construction of Amy's and Sethe's worlds, we observe that race and class
do *not* determine intelligence or talent, but that they do limit and, all
too frequently, destroy the creative impulse.[11]

As young girls growing up in their separate spheres of bondage, Amy
and Sethe are self-made and self-defined. Prior to her break for freedom
and as an adolescent, Sethe had no black female role models, being the
only female slave on the Garner farm. Amy's condition suggests that she
also has grown up without the care of a mother figure and has had little
time for personal development. "Most times," Amy says, "I'm feeding
stock before light and don't get to sleep till way after dark comes" (80).
She remembers a song her mother taught her, which she sings as though
to reassure herself and Sethe of a safe night's sleep. The contrastive images of Sethe's and Amy's mothers are stark: Amy remembers a lullaby:
"That's my mama's song. She taught me it" (81), while Sethe's memory
of her mother is a mark seared in the flesh: "Right on her rib was a circle
and a cross burnt right in the skin" (61). Mark Ledbetter describes this
scar as "a welcomed mark of distinction, painful and necessary, where
little distinction exists . . . from the perspective of the enslaver" (43). The
narrative underscores these contrasting maternal images—a lullaby embedded in Amy's memory and a flesh wound repeated on Sethe's back.
Maternal memories notwithstanding, without present mother figures,
Sethe and Amy have had to learn, as best they could, what it means to be
women.

These young women are nevertheless fugitives. Amy has run away
from a plantation in Kentucky, where she had lived for about sixteen
years, working off her mother's indenture: "My mama worked for these
here people to pay for her passage. But then she had me and since she died
right after, well, they said I had to work for em to pay it off" (33). Though
victimized by this economic system and physically beaten, Amy recognizes that her indenture was markedly different from Sethe's enslavement: "I had me some whippings, but I don't remember nothing like this.
Mr. Buddy had a right evil hand too. Whip you for looking at him straight.
Sure would. I looked right at him one time and he hauled off and threw
the poker at me. Guess he knew what I was a-thinking" (79). The subtle
contrast here is Amy's ability to "look right at" Mr. Buddy in contrast to
the slaves' command never to look directly at whites. Amy's subsequent
remarks implicitly point toward their racial differences: "Maybe you

should of stayed where you was, Lu. I can see by your back why you didn't ha ha. Whoever planted that tree beat Mr. Buddy by a mile. Glad I ain't you" (79). Is Amy glad she isn't a black girl? A nigger? Is the "you" Amy interprets the reader's "you"?

The word "nigger" moves easily on Amy's tongue; it is part of her social discourse that suggests insensitivity as well as naïveté. These contradictions are underscored several times in this scene. Amy's discussion about "a old nigger girl" who "don't know nothing" but "sews stuff . . . real fine lace but can't barely stick two words together" conflates what Amy has been taught and what her own observations contradict. Her reference to the older black woman as a girl and her insistence to Sethe, "She don't know nothing, just like you" (80), should not escape readers. The language of disrespect and callousness is overlaid with Amy's admiration for the woman's skill in making lace. And what are we to make of Amy's "[kneeling] to massage [Sethe's] swollen feet"? "Give these one more real good rub" is countered by "Don't up and die on me in the night, you hear? I don't want to see your ugly black face hankering over me" (82). Amy's soothing hands counter her potentially divisive words. The unself-conscious sincerity of her deeds—set against her (un)conscious linguistic posturing—is both disconcerting and comforting to Sethe. "I hear" and "I'll do what I can" are Sethe's responses. Amy's obvious delight that Sethe made it through the night is undercut by her language: "Looks like the devil—but you made it through. Come down here, Jesus, Lu made it through." Amy, deservedly, credits herself for Sethe's making it through since Sethe herself "never expected to see another thing in this world." "That's because of me. I'm good at sick things" is Amy's praise for herself and relief that Sethe has helped Amy get through the dark night (82). Amy's alternating stance between the role of a white woman and the role of a mutually dependent fugitive invites readers' collusion and critique.

Like Amy, Sethe has been a surrogate for a woman in bondage. She was purchased at age thirteen to replace a slave, Baby Suggs, who eventually became her mother-in-law. And like Amy, Sethe knew very little of her mother, but what she remembers is in stark contrast to Amy's memories: "I didn't see [my mother] but a few times out in the fields and once when she was working indigo. By the time I woke up in the morning, she was in line. If the moon was bright they worked by its light. Sunday she slept like a stick. She must of nursed me two or three weeks— that's the way the others did. Then she went back in rice and I sucked from another woman whose job it was" (60).

This adumbration of Amy's and Sethe's backgrounds in terms of age, conditions of servitude, and sensibilities emphasizes the similarities between these young women rather than their racial differences. Their commonalities allow them to engage in conversations that reveal the persons they are "inside." The most significant aspect of their meeting is the contradiction between what is said and what is actually done; their meeting suggests that external appearances such as race, class, and habits of speaking are not the final judge of one individual's potential for compassion toward an individual of another race. Amy and Sethe are exemplars of Morrison's notion of one kind of interracial relationship between women.

This scenario also stresses gender bonding and highlights both women's knowledge and experience surrounding the female body and childbirth: "How old are you, Lu? I been bleeding for four years but I ain't having nobody's baby. Won't catch me sweating milk" (83). Although Amy has had no experience with childbirth, after her initial shock of the premature birthing, she quickly recovers and responds "appropriately and well" (85)—at times instinctively: "'Push!' screamed Amy. 'Pull,' whispered Sethe" (84). The birth scene implies in some respects that women are midwives by virtue of their gender. The conversation prior to the birth and Amy's instinctive scream for Sethe to push and Sethe's urging Amy to pull seem to define the moment as a feminine one: two women doing what most women have traditionally been thought to do naturally. The birthing scene also establishes a permanent bond between them when Sethe chooses to name the child they delivered Denver. Sethe's decision is more than gratitude; it is a reminder of a white woman who jeopardized her freedom in order to assist Sethe at a moment of crisis and potential death. These scenes of female bonding call attention to the contradiction between what is expected and what actually occurs and challenges readers to rethink received notions of racial and class differences.

Although these circumstances diminish the racial and class differences between Amy and Sethe, we are reminded that once the women's shared ordeal ends their differences are reinscribed in Amy's gestures and language. Her parting comments reimpose their racial and potential class differences. "Lift[ing] her chin," Amy quizzes Sethe to be sure that she will tell the newborn about Amy's role in her birth. "You gonna tell her? . . . You better tell her. You hear? Say Miss Amy Denver. Of Boston" (85). Amy's posture, her tone of voice, and her invocation of the title "Miss" bring their encounter back to its beginning. "Miss" invokes both race and class distinctions based solely on the color of Amy's skin since there is little difference between their relative backgrounds and present condition. The narrative alerts us to other realities concerning their futures by calling attention to their individual expectations. In bringing us back to Amy's dream of a life in Boston as a "Miss Amy Denver" and Sethe's hope of crossing "one mile of dark water, which would have to be split with one oar in a useless boat ["full of holes"] against a current dedicated to the Mississippi one hundred miles away" (83), the narrative suggests that, as a poor white girl, Amy's prospects are not altogether unfounded. She can expect and, no doubt, will receive help in her flight to freedom, even though it is highly questionable whether she will ever be a "proper" Boston lady. Sethe, a black female fugitive, has little prospects for a brighter future, even if she survives the river crossing. And if she does survive—unlike Amy, who had earlier reminded Sethe that no one was searching for her (Amy)—Sethe still faces the possibility of being overtaken by her owner and returned to slavery. In spite of Sethe's miraculous crossing into the free state of Ohio, she is subsequently discovered and is rescued from a second life in slavery by killing one of her children and injuring the others. After this daring act of insurgency, Sethe remains free because her owner considers her and her children to be "damaged goods": "Right off it was clear, to schoolteacher especially, that there was nothing there to claim. The three (now four—because she'd had the one coming when she cut) pickaninnies they had hoped were alive and well enough to take back to Kentucky, take back and raise properly to do the work Sweet Home desperately needed, were not" (149).

The juxtaposition of Sethe's and Amy's lives moves the narrative beyond their present encounter to embrace larger social and nationalistic issues. The birth scene functions as a tropological event for the rebirth of nationhood between blacks and whites, between North and South. At the site of Denver's birth—the Ohio River—the border between North and South, between freedom and enslavement, between life and death, the narrative holds out the promise that separation based on differences may be overcome. Homi Bhabha has written that "it is in the emergence of the interstice—the overlap and displacement of domains of difference—that the intersubjective and collective experiences of *nationness*, community interests, or cultural values are negotiated" (2). Or, as Sharon Montieth suggests, "Interracial friendships work to expose the context in which friendship may be seen as transgressive, trespassing the borders of what is socially expected or countenanced" (2–3). In this emergent cooperative encounter and potential for friendship between Sethe and Amy, Morrison exposes the tenuous lines that separate individuals and lays the groundwork for broader and more lasting cross-racial and cross-cultural friendships.

Issues of race and class are at the core of *Tar Baby*. Morrison's sche-
ma for representing these categories differs vastly from the techniques
she employs in "Recitatif" and *Beloved*. Jadine Childs (*Tar Baby*) both
claims and disclaims her allegiance to the African American community in particular and the American and European communities in general. Her inability to be both African and American leads her from her na-
tal community toward the white world in order to be one of "them."
Frances E. W. Harper stages this ambiguous position in *Iola Leroy* (1892),
but Harper's female protagonist has no difficulty choosing between the
white and black worlds, having lived in both worlds and having understood the negative consequences of choosing white. Iola's brother correctly states Iola's position: "She is not one who can't be white and won't be
black" (278). One character in *Tar Baby* (Gideon) says of Jadine, whom
he refers to as "yalla," "It's hard for them not to be white people. Hard.
I'm telling you. . . . Some try, but most don't make it" (155). Or, as the
narrator in Gayl Jones's *Mosquito* puts it, "When people be running from
them stereotypes based on some kinda reality a lot of times they be running from they own culture, they be running from theyselves" (44).[12]

Jadine's forays into Western culture and her seeming integration into
Western society represent one of Morrison's fictional moments that,
when read from Jadine's perspective, may lead us to conclude that she
has "made it" in a white world—that she has breached the barriers that
so many African Americans have found impenetrable. Yet a closer scrutiny of Jadine and the white world in which she moves with ostensible
grace and confidence reveals that it is more facade than reality. Her doubts
about her engagement to Ryk, a wealthy Frenchman, and her denuncia-
tion and mockery of African and African American cultures attest to her
inculcation of those negative aspects of Western culture—its denigration
of nonwhite cultures and its particular contempt for African Americans.
Jadine's attitude can best be described by what Joyce King calls "dysconscious racism"—the belief that all norms and realities based upon a white
Anglo-Saxon weltanschauung are the only correct worldview (135). Or,
to borrow from Ngugi wa Thiong'o, it can be argued that Jadine has internalized the beliefs and norms of the colonizer and has accepted the
"deliberate undervaluing" of the "culture" and "art" of black peoples (16).
Morrison's theory of what constitutes a *house* versus a *home* may serve
as a trope for Jadine's rejection of her "home" for a "house." Morrison
states she is "an already—and always—raced writer," but one who refuses

to "reproduce the master's voice and its assumptions of the all-knowing law of the white father" ("Home" 4)—a refusal to reject the racial home for a racist house. *Tar Baby,* if we accept Morrison's version of home and homelessness, is a narrative about race, racism, and racelessness. Judy-lyn Ryan points out that Jadine "is not only rootless but, in receiving a Eurocentric education, has been *grafted* onto a self-alienating cultural base from which to view her own experiences and those of other African peoples" (78). These simultaneous readings of Jadine provide readers with clues for understanding the ambiguity of *Tar Baby* and the complex di-lemma the narrative poses for Jadine—be all she can be or be black and proud? The text implies multiple choices, and Jadine's journey is to de-termine the authentic, self-fulfilling choices for her—choices that will enable her to feel at home in the worlds in which she moves and works.

Jadine is often characterized as a dual orphan: she is orphaned at a young age and reared by her aunt and uncle; she becomes a cultural or-phan when she is educated in a white world under the auspices of a white benefactor. These two factors are crucial to her racial identity, driving her inner conflicts about who she is and where she belongs. Morrison has remarked that Jadine "is cut off," that she lacks certain qualities her Aunt Ondine possesses, that she is not "a complete woman. She doesn't have that quality because she can avoid it." Jadine is part "new capitalistic, modern American black which is what everybody thought was the ulti-mate in integration. To produce Jadine, that's what it was for." Such a production can be "danger[ous]," Morrison contends, since "it cannot replace certain essentials from the past." Jadine "cannot nurture and be a career woman" (Ruas 104–5). Jadine chooses a career; and when she tells the phantom women she also has breasts, it is clear from the narrative details that her breasts are an extension of her eroticized and fetishized body with "six centimeters of cleavage supported (more or less) by silver lamé" (116). Jadine's eroticized breasts in the photograph are reinforced by her masturbation on the sealskin coat: "She lifted herself up a little and let her nipples brush the black hairs, back and forth" (91), and she is embarrassed as she watches Son as he looks at the coat and wonders if "he could see the print of her nipples" (114).[13] It is crucial to note the conflict between Jadine as a nurturer and as a career woman since the bare-breasted women echo Sojourner Truth's purported exposure of her breasts not only to prove her femininity ("I have borne thirteen children"), but more importantly to tout her "career" ("I have ploughed and plant-ed, gathered into barns, and no man could head me! And ain't I a wom-an?") (qtd. in Conboy et al. 231).[14] But Jadine never considers nurturing as an option; in fact, she bitterly resists what she perceives to be her aunt and uncle's desire for her to nurse them in their old age.

These identity issues are framed within an artificial world—"this place [L'Arbe de la Croix] dislocates everything" (284)—and within artificial relationships that expose Jadine's vulnerability to false allegiances and untenable communal connections. Jadine's affair with Son concludes with her cavalier dismissal of him as a "cultural throwback" with a "white-folks-black-folks primitivism" (275). Yet she is *uncertain* about the motives of the white man she wants to marry. She is *certain*, however, that the one "desperate to marry her was exciting and smart and fun and sexy." Still she worries "if the person he wants to marry is me or a black girl." Even more problematic for her is the possibility that "if it isn't me he wants, but any black girl who looks like me, talks and acts like me, what will happen when he finds out that I hate ear hoops, that I don't have to straighten my hair, that Mingus puts me to sleep, that sometimes I want to get out of my skin and be only the person inside me—not American—not black—just me?" (48).[15] Her desire to turn inward and away from blackness and African-Americanness is an expressed wish to be disconnected from her most immediate communities.[16]

Jadine's statement reads like a desire to abnegate blackness and become the Westernized "orphan," and it also brings her closer to the trope of the soldier-ant queen who "seals herself off from all society and eats her own wing muscles until she bears her eggs" (291). Stated another way, Jadine *"was* the safety she longed for" (290). This "safety" is delusional: she cannot exist within herself alone. And as much as she would like to believe that she can, her questions about who she is in relation to others are more about her own self-absorption and stubborn conviction that her education and her small fortune of "$1,940 in the bank, $5,000 in Paris and connections" (230) will enable her to be "the person inside her mind"; this is Cartesian rationalization, not the reality of a black woman in the Western world. Until she can move beyond solipsism, her return to Paris will lead to further confusion about who she is. This fact does not mean that Son is necessarily correct when he asserts that "people don't mix races; they abandon them" (270).

In her presumed independence and self-reliance (eating her own wings and cutting herself off from those who nurtured her), Jadine's choice, as Philip Page argues, is "devalued" and undermined by the narrative discourse (127–28). Michael, the son of her white benefactor, had raised the question of her "studying art history at that snotty school instead of . . . organizing or something" or "abandoning history . . . [her] people" (72). Jadine, with a touch of bitter irony, tells her benefactor, "I knew the life I was leaving. It wasn't like what he thought: all grits and natural grace." When Michael tries to make her apologize "for liking 'Ave Maria' better than gospel music," she asserts that "Picasso *is* better than an Itumba mask. The fact that he was intrigued by them is proof of *his* genius, not the mask-makers'" (74). She fails to see the contradiction in her own language when, referring to black art shows, she thinks "of all those black art shows mounted two or three times a year in the States. The junior high school sculpture, the illustration-type painting. Eighty percent ludicrous and ten percent *derivative* to the point of *mimicry*" (74; emphasis added). Her denigration of the black community evidences her inculcation of Western hegemony that sees little of value in African and African American culture. Jadine's statements alert readers to the fact that a black woman inadequately grounded in black culture or totally immersed in Western culture may not necessarily live securely in either.

Jadine's social world is exclusive, even though it includes blacks and whites. After college, "when she traveled her society included blacks and whites in profusion, but the black people she knew wanted what she wanted—either steadily and carefully . . . or uproariously and flashy." And "with white people the rules were even simpler. She needed only to be stunning, and to convince them she was not as smart as they were. Say the obvious, ask stupid questions, laugh with abandon, look interested, and light up at any display of their humanity if they showed it" (126–27). Is Jadine's description a commentary on young black women such as herself? Or is the text signifying on both groups—each using the other for self-serving intentions? Through Jadine we see Morrison's concern about "the impact of race on the romance of community and individuality" ("Home" 9). *Tar Baby* also points out that no individual can live securely without some affective links to community and reminds us that Jadine's annoyance with Valerian's amused acceptance of Son stems from the fact that Valerian may not appreciate "the difference between one Black and another" and that he may "think we're all . . ." (125). Jadine does not complete the sentence. Is it because, as much as she would rather not think so, she fears that Valerian, like her French fiancé, makes no distinctions among blacks? This fear is what keeps Jadine and other successful blacks "orphans" in the Western world.

Jadine's ostensible self-sufficiency crumbles under the press of her sexual craving that contrasts sharply with the eroticized body portrayed in a French magazine. Her masturbation upon the fur coat given to her by her French lover attests to her erotic urges and presages her sexual trysts with Son. As she sinks into the sealskin coat, she "close[s] her eyes and imagine[s]" herself "sinking into a blackness." Lying "spread-eagle on the fur . . . she licks it and trembles more" (113). Jadine's response to the fur coat—a symbol of her desire for the privileges and promises of the white world and the jouisance associated with Son, "So very hard to forget the man who fucked like a star" (292)—has an equivalent moment in *The Bluest Eye* in Pecola's erotic responses to the Mary Jane candies: "Three pennies had bought her nine lovely orgasms with Mary Jane. Lovely Mary Jane for whom a candy is named" (43). Jadine's overwhelming desire not to be just a part of the white world and not to be thought of as black, which is another way of saying she wants to *be* white, is tantamount to Pecola's desire for blue eyes. Jadine also admits that she is jealous because Son chose Margaret's closet for hiding rather than hers, and much to her chagrin she realizes that she has been "competing with [Margaret] for rape" (186), a further indication of her view of herself as a "white" woman and her attraction to Son, despite his crudeness and his filthy body.

A compendium of differences coalesce at the Christmas dinner when Valerian, the presumptive "master" of L'Arbe de la Croix, invites the household—including his servants and Son, the unlawful intruder—to "sit down and have the dinner among ourselves." This scene highlights the separate spheres and unequal relationships among these characters. The opportunity for "a special and intimate relationship with his employer pleased [Sydney] more than disconcerted him" because "what was unthinkable and undesirable in Philadelphia was not so on that island" (195). More importantly for Sydney, who had been angered by Valerian's acceptance of Son as a houseguest, is that "it leveled . . . the invitation Mr. Street had extended to Son when everybody thought he was a burglar" (195–96). What appears to be an occasion for de-hierarchizing their relationships erupts into accusations and revelations: Margaret reminds Son that when she discovered him hiding in her closet what she saw was "a big black man"—the stereotypical black male some white women see as potential rapists; Ondine accuses Margaret of child abuse; Valerian accuses the servants who work in the yard and laundry room of stealing his apples; Valerian also accuses Ondine of disrespecting his wife; Ondine in turn accuses Valerian of not telling her he had fired the accused servants. When Sydney comes to his wife's defense, Street retorts, "I'm beholding to a cook for the welfare of two people she hated." Ondine fires back, "I may be a cook, Mr. Street, but I'm a person too" (207). The swift deterioration of what is ostensibly an occasion for this group to set aside those things that traditionally divide them (race, class, and gender) causes them to revert to old habits and customary behavior. When Jadine asks why Valerian's experiment in egalitarianism failed, Son suggests "that white folks and black folks should not sit down and eat together." His response alerts the reader to the intertextuality of the scene—a critique of Martin Luther King's dream of a table of universal brotherhood, especially when Son states, "They should work together sometimes, but they should not eat together or live together or sleep together. Do any of those personal things in life" (210). The insertion of the word "personal" gives double meaning to Son's remark: it expresses his displeasure with the immediate situation and the novel's suggestion that it will take more than an occasional dinner among people of different backgrounds to overcome years of entrenched prejudices and racism.

Son's contentions are that racial disharmonies in this country can never rise to intimacy and mutual respect. The narrative clearly indicates that racial lines have been crossed, but, like Ondine's telling her boss to keep his wife out of "my kitchen," the reality is that many whites still have the choice to retreat to their positions of privilege. "*Your* kitchen? *Your* help?" (207)—Street's recognition that twice his authority has been undermined comes as a surprise even to himself. All politeness and repressed racism erupt. Ondine calls Margaret a "crazy white freak"; Margaret calls her a "nigger bitch." Ondine leaves the room asserting, "I am the woman in this house. None other," while Margaret tries to cover her years of child abuse: "I am not one of those women in the *National Enquirer*" (208–9). All the subterranean prejudices and anxieties these characters have held for years disrupt the intended peaceful scenario of one ostensibly happy household.

The relationship between Margaret and Ondine turns out to be as tenuous and temporary as the relationships between Amy and Sethe and Twyla and Roberta. It develops out of Margaret's need for companionship, a need engendered by her husband's neglect and her conviction that her beauty is not enough to sustain their marriage. She lacks the social skills presumed essential to the class into which she married. Beyond the eruption of political and social issues, this scene condenses the history of race and class and gendered relations in this country. Valerian, the patriarch, momentarily reclaims his status of master, while the others are reminded of their places in relation to him and to one another. In the end, however, the old order is repeated—the white patriarch reaches a point when he can no longer feed himself and is at the mercy of his aging and faithful servant: Sydney "took the knife and fork from Valerian, broke open the steaming potato . . . blew on it and then held it in front of Valerian's mouth" (286). Here we see again the intersection of race and need—the elder servant's dependence on his master for employment, despite his frailty, and the old master's reliance on his servant to care for him, despite his economic wealth. This scenario posits a distinction without a difference.

Morrison offers her readers multiple answers to the dilemma posed by difference, answers yoked to her readers' individual responses to her narratives. She is suggesting that such conflicts are at the center of many failed attempts by blacks and whites in the United States to achieve relationships that recognize difference while honoring their common humanity. The disruption of Martin Luther King Jr.'s dream, implicit in this scene, is Morrison's unwillingness to grant a facile solution to the complex issues surrounding difference. Margaret's scream about the black male in her closet and Valerian's assertion of authority—however hollow—compel an adjustment to the notion that race and class differences can be abolished by simply placing in the same room a group of people from diverse backgrounds. Jessica Benjamin's assertion that it is "difficult to attain a notion of difference, being unlike, without giving up a sense of commonality, of being a 'like' human being" (50) is applicable here.

With the publication of *Tar Baby* and, subsequently, "Recitatif" and *Beloved,* Morrison was prepared to insert in her fiction a seriously playful dimension and frontally challenge her readers to be more deeply involved in her narrative play. In these texts race is no longer an underlying issue; it is central to Morrison's aesthetics because whites are no longer marginal characters; they now have much more direct and sustained relationships with blacks. Race now implicates the reader far more directly in the narrative outcomes. Race is both present and absent, which is to say that Morrison has self-consciously inserted racialized bodies into her texts, in part to share her desire to have her readers recognize the "difficulties of signing race," that is, inscribing race, "while designing racelessness," or constructing narratives that deliberately throw race into question as an essential mark of identity ("Home" 8).

3 "Slips of Sorrow": Narrating the Pain of Difference and the Rhetoric of Healing

> Black women have held, have been given . . . the cross.
> They don't walk near it. They're often on it. And
> they've borne that, I think, extremely well.
>
> —Toni Morrison, conversation with Robert Stepto

In the preceding chapter I considered Morrison's concern with the politics of physical and social differences and their effects upon intersubjective relations. In this chapter I consider the external stigma of difference from the internal perspectives of characters for whom difference induces psychic trauma. I move from intersubjective relations involving difference to Morrison's concern with the intrasubjective consequences of difference, the psychodrama demarcating certain characters' lives. In shifting the focus from Morrison's concern with the politics of exterior features of difference—observable markers such as phenotypic features and physical deformations—to the internal pressures, emotional and psychological, I hope to show how certain characters, perceived solely as victims and objects of alienation, attempt to subvert the objectifying gaze and thwart further victimization by asserting some measure of control over their lives. How do women survive under hostile and psychologically debilitating conditions? Do ancestral female figures offer potential solutions for survival, or do they merely point toward a continuum of black women's internal struggles prompted by race and gender. In her critique of the African American community's response to physical and mental difference, does Morrison suggest alternative models for recognizing and coping with alienation induced by conditions over which black women may or may not have control? Morrison's construction of suffering as one expression of African American women's responses to interracial, intraracial, and interpersonal relations provides some answers to these questions by demonstrating how those women confront the interior struggles that differentiate them from and situate them within the circle of women in the larger society.

In 1968 William H. Grier and Price M. Cobbs published an influential study of anger and its devastating effects on African Americans. These psychiatrists spoke of "the handicap of being born black," of the vicious "reality of being alternately attacked, ignored, then singled out for some cruel and undeserved punishment" that surely "must extract its toll" (30). Citing, among others, a case involving a woman named Bertha, who believed that she was "a black, ugly, ignorant, dirty little girl who could be loved by no one" (7), Grier and Cobbs concluded that "black women have a nearly bottomless pit of self-depreciation into which they can drop when depressed. The well is prepared by society and stands waiting, a prefabricated pit which they had no hand in fashioning" (9). I mention Grier and Cobbs's *Black Rage* because at the time of its publication Morrison was working on her manuscript for *The Bluest Eye;* she may well have read the book, and black rage may have influenced her treatment of the anger and anguish of black existence.[1]

In her concern with identity politics, Morrison constructs the self as an interior space in relation to exterior features of difference. In constructing the psychic effects of difference as mediated in the desire for intersubjectivity, Morrison brings into sharper focus the efforts of those perceived as different to heal their psychic hurts by scrutinizing and acquiescing to or altering the conditions under which their difference marginalizes and/ or alienates them. What is often overlooked, Morrison's narratives suggest, is the interior suffering of the subjects inside the manifest beings the public sees. Or to paraphrase Twyla's recognition of Maggie's humanity, we sometimes forget that there is "somebody" inside the physical body ("Recitatif" 245). Is Pecola merely a manifestation of madness engendered by verbal and physical abuse? Or are we to search for some deeper level of her humanity masked by that madness? In constructing the interiority of difference within the African American community, Morrison challenges the prevailing perception that white society must bear primary responsibility for African Americans' suffering, and she urges African Americans to consider their own complicity in and contribution to the

suffering within the black community. While African Americans' negative attitudes and insensitive behavior toward one another may often find
their roots in the historical treatment of blacks by whites in the United
States, ultimately, Morrison's fiction implies, a partial solution to mitigating the psychic trauma of alienation within African America lies with
African Americans themselves. But, as Orlando Patterson observes, one
must be wary of placing responsibility within the African American community because so many African Americans still view racism as the cul-
prit: "Any suggestion that an Afro-American person might be responsible, even in some minor way, for his or her condition invites the knee-jerk
response that one is blaming the victim." Although I disagree with Patterson's fundamental argument that at this juncture "relations between or-
dinary Afro-Americans and Euro-Americans are, in fact, better than they
have ever been" (2), I agree with his statement that some African Americans attribute the problems in their community to racism alone. Morrison resists the temptation to blame white society by refusing to relegate
black suffering to external racism alone. She casts a wide net that ensnares
numerous culprits. She depicts subjects victimized by individual and societal forces and the inner and outer forces these subjects rely on to endure and/or recover from such victimizations.

While this chapter focuses on individual characters, these individuals are metonyms for the many African American women whose suffering comes from white racism and from the insensitivity of those African
Americans sometimes emulating and repeating the wrongs of the past.
It is easy to dismiss individuals like Pecola and Violet as disquieting forces
to be pitied, ignored, isolated—even derided—rather than as subjects
subtly and overtly pleading for help in dealing with their demons. To state
it differently, we may ask how those who seem powerless to describe their
demons, though they may express them in aberrant ways, compel and
deserve our compassion and understanding, not our pity and condemna-
tion. Although each of the characters discussed here represents a different form of interior pain, cumulatively they share a common bond of
residing in a community that must assume a great deal of responsibility
for their condition.

In the final chapter of *Jazz*, the narrator remarks, "Pain. I seem to
have an affection, a kind of sweettooth for it. . . . I break lives to prove I
can mend them back again." Despite claims to inventive and destructive powers, this narrator admits discomfort and "feel[s] a bit false." It[2]
asks, "What, I wonder, what would I be without a few brilliant spots of
blood to ponder? Without aching words that set, then miss the mark?"
(219). This example from *Jazz* is irresistibly seductive in its momentary

figuration of the author—Toni Morrison—appropriating the voice of the narrator to slyly answer the question, "'Why are your books so melancholy, so sad? Why don't you ever write about something that works, about relationships that are healthy?'" To which Morrison has responded, "I write in what . . . could be called the tragic mode in which there is some catharsis and revelation" (LeClair 125). The fictional process that permits Morrison to manipulate the narrative voice is especially effective in *Jazz* because the narrator has already revealed itself as a shapeshifter. In the passage cited above, this protean narrator engages in a double-voiced discourse, aligning itself with the author and speaking as the author might speak outside the text.[3] The voice is also Morrison's way of reserving the right to explore pain of whatever description: that of individuals alienated on the basis of physical differences and/or psychological damage. In this instance, Morrison appropriates the narrator's voice to state her position on the relationship between the writer and the construction of pain—to assert that when she writes about pain she must have some shared knowledge of her characters' sufferings. The narrator/implied author does admit that "the pain is theirs [the characters']. I share it, don't I? . . . But it is another way" (219). This other "way" is the writer's way of converting pain into a trope as complex as the characters whose experiences reflect that pain.

Morrison's textualization and metaphorization of black women in pain allow us to read their condition within two life worlds: the real and the imaginative. In all of her fictional texts to date, Morrison has thematized black women's endurance, subversion, and transcendence of pain. She has used memory—voiced and unvoiced—as a technique for articulating what Eddie George has called the "broken voice[s]" (qtd. in hooks, *Yearning* 146) within which bell hooks urges us to "hear the pain" and the "speech of suffering." But, hooks continues, the memory of pain must "serve to illuminate and transform the present" (*Yearning* 147). It is through her characters' memory and transformations that Morrison brings their pain to the attention of her readers.

In her essay "Speaking in Tongues," Mae G. Henderson affirms that "black women writers have encoded oppression as a discursive dilemma" and have used "silence as an important element of this code" (24). Morrison's fiction encompasses and transcends this discursive dilemma and evidences her desire to disrupt such silence. Her fictional replication of black women's subjection, victimization, and scapegoating also enables the possibilities to subvert and diminish these modes of dominance by ensuring that black women's voices are heard. Thus Morrison constructs black women as individuals trapped in a spiral of racist and sexist practices that not only constrict and marginalize them but also warp their psyches. While these women-centered narratives articulate pain inflicted by subjection, rejection, and loss, they also depict the willed assertiveness of women who refuse to be silenced or oppressed.[4] While the women in Morrison's fiction endure and sometimes transcend different kinds of pain, the sources of their pain are often similar: pain accumulates to them from their multiple subject positions and often results from poverty and abandonment, or from parental, spousal, communal, and institutional abuse. Eventually, their sufferings reach us as facts of black women's lives and lead us to read their lives in terms of the strength and stamina they need to exist in these multiple positions. These women are linked by their determination to explore, to live in and through their suffering.

Narratives by African American women, according to Aaron David Gresson III, "typically exemplify [a] rhetoric of being" that tries to "engage a listener in a shared vision of each other as sensible and sensitive Blacks." These two rhetorical visions emerge as part of black women's narrative projects when the "sensible appears in the urgent concern for personal survival and well-being" and the "sensitive appears in an acknowledgment that one is . . . Black and therefore ought to do something for someone in need—some oppressed Other." Gresson notes "a constant, though not always continual, tension" in this rhetoric of being (23). Such tensions define many of Morrison's female characters attempting to negotiate sensibly and sensitively in a world that often denies their autonomous and personal agency. While Morrison exposes the vulnerabilities of these tortured women, she also reveals their drive toward human attachments that honor their self-worth and recognize that separation can initiate and fuel psychic disorders.

In *The Bluest Eye*, Morrison depicts several sources of black women's pain: old age, death, and the collective memories of suffering and triumph; middle age and thwarted desires; and childhood with its concomitant hurts. Just as Claudia and the omniscient narrator have primary responsibility to recount scenes of suffering, so do other characters provide direct access to their troubled interior worlds. The novel also records black women's discrete and collective experiences that negatively impact their lives. Aunt Jimmy's illness and death provide opportunities for women to reiterate their lived experiences as objects of the community's power and subjection. These women, who seem to have "edge[d] into life from the back door. Becoming . . . "with only one group from whom they do not have to take orders—their children (109), offer us some insights into familial and personal relationships through the conflation of black women's pain with Aunt Jimmy's illness, or with what M'Dear, the "competent midwife" and "decisive diagnostician," terms a "cold in [her] womb" (108). The literal and metaphorical coalesce in Aunt Jimmy's womb: it is both the repository of physical life and the symbolic site of femaleness; it is at once the organ of fertility and the sign of loss and separation—the source of connection and disconnection between the mother and child. The womb can bear fruit and signal barrenness. So the cold in Aunt Jimmy's womb accrues polysemy as it signals Aunt Jimmy's death and the beginning of Cholly's independence.

After M'Dear's pronouncement and departure, Aunt Jimmy is visited by two other friends, Miss Alice and Mrs. Gaines, whose "voices blended into a threnody of nostalgia about pain. Rising and falling, complex in harmony, uncertain in pitch, but constant in the recitative of pain" (109). Aunt Jimmy's deathbed becomes the site of memory and loss—a moment for recollection and release. The three women recite a condensed history of pain that includes perseverance and a necessary distinction between what *was* and what *is*. The element of triumph stems from their having endured the miseries of their youth and middle age: "They hugged the memories of illness to their bosoms . . . licked their lips and clucked their tongues in fond remembrance of pains they had endured" (109). Their pain is expressed in a pre-eulogy for Aunt Jimmy and a shared knowledge that constitutes both litany and praisesong: "childbirth, rheumatism, croup, sprains, backaches, piles. All of the bruises they had collected from moving about the earth—harvesting, cleaning, hoisting, pitching, stooping, kneeling, picking—always with young ones underfoot" (109). The narrator hastens to add details that render this pain race and gender specific. These women have risen above the humiliations and pain, even though "everybody in the world was in a position to give them orders. White women said, 'Do this.' White children said, 'Give me that.' White men said, 'Come here.' Black men said, 'Lay down.' . . . When white men beat their men, they [the women] cleaned up the blood and went home to receive abuse from the victim" (109–10). The violence these women have endured from their own men invites our scrutiny of the double bind in which African American women often find themselves: objects of male abuse and surrogates for white men who go unpunished by their victims—black men.

Aunt Jimmy's death opens a space for black women to reflect on their lives, and it is an occasion to assess black women's lives, a process the narrator encapsulates in one sentence: "The lives of these old black women were synthesized in their eyes—a purée of tragedy and humor, wickedness and serenity, truth and fantasy" (110). The passage stresses both suffering and pleasure. Instead of sentimentalizing their pain, the narrator valorizes their strength and perseverance. Margaret Wilkerson notes that this description "implies the rise and fall of the women's voices and the nuances of their dialogue." Wilkerson hears in "the tone of their speech . . . the ritual of the wake," which she terms "a muted prelude to the joy of the funeral banquet that follows" (187). After Aunt Jimmy's interment, the narrator comments that "there was grief over the waste of life, the stunned wonder at the ways of God, and the restoration of nature in the graveyard" (113). The living are left with the pain and emptiness of death. The litany concludes with the acceptance of suffering and death and the continuation of life. For Aunt Jimmy's female friends, one solution to pain and suffering is living with the knowledge of both and holding on in spite of them. The narrator's summation of this illuminating moment—"Thus the banquet [at the home of the deceased is] the exultation, the harmony, the acceptance of physical frailty, joy in the termination of misery. Laughter, relief, a steep hunger for food" (113)—suggests that the desire to live overwhelms the shadow of death.

Aunt Jimmy's narrative, part of Pauline's and Pecola's histories by way of Charlie Breedlove's, is located in the South, while Geraldine's narrative, deeply rooted in her Southern past, is set in the North. The narratives establish a tenuous dichotomy, one that marks superficial differences because at the core Geraldine cannot escape the world of pain many other black women have known, her well-groomed body and comfortable house notwithstanding. In contrast to Aunt Jimmy's narrative that takes place in "spring," Geraldine's narrative is set in winter. She is, by implication, associated with decay and deadness. She is depicted as part of a large category of women who share her vision and sensibility, women who "go to land-grant colleges, normal schools, and learn," among other things, "how to behave . . . how to get rid of the funkiness. The dread funkiness of passion, the funkiness of nature, the funkiness of the wide range of human emotions" (68). While the women at Aunt Jimmy's wake recognize and claim the sources of their pain, Geraldine denies the reality of her condition through her obsessive neatness, a defense against her psychic tension. This denial transmutes to internalized anguish and repressed anger over her blackness as a mark of limitation and confinement to a black existence The weight of this reality causes Geraldine to project her internal struggles with blackness onto her son and onto Pecola, who represents what Madonne M. Miner describes as "a series of signs, symbolic configuration"—a composite of all the negative baggage Geraldine associates with blackness—"everything ugly, dirty and degrading" (185).

Geraldine's appropriation of bourgeois values—or what Ann Cook, at the time, called "white values in black face" (149)—masks the anger and anguish associated with her blackness, a condition she tries to transcend by keeping a well-groomed son and a spotless house, not unlike Helene Wright's "oppressive neatness" and "curdled scorn" of Sula (*Sula* 19).[5] Geraldine's behavior also belies the exterior manifestations of what Pecola sees as a "pretty milk-brown lady in the pretty gold-and-green house" (76). What Pecola does not recognize is, as Gurleen Grewal remarks, that Geraldine's "virtuous stability is built upon the repression of her embodied blackness" (29). Pecola's surprise and confusion over Geraldine's outburst result from the contradiction between Geraldine's appearance and her actions. It is evident from her unprovoked verbal flailing at Pecola that Geraldine is reacting to something deep within herself—repressed anger and frustration prompted by racism that compel her to suffer overtly as a black woman while she exists internally as a white woman. Pecola sees Geraldine's exteriority in the interior of her house, but we see beyond Pecola's vision into Geraldine's lifelong suffering, as well as into Pecola's unarticulated desire as she gazes at "the blue eyes in the black face" of Geraldine's cat (*Bluest* 75). Pecola is more than mesmerized by the cat's blue eyes; she sees in them the possibility for her wish fulfillment.

Gunilla T. Kester has noted that Pecola's self-concept might have been radically different had she received "more support" from her community (*Writing the Subject* 77), an argument equally applicable to Pecola's mother. The text juxtaposes Pecola's desire for blue eyes with her mother's nostalgia for a gone world and lost love. Pauline's narrative, like the voices at Aunt Jimmy's, is set in the spring. Pauline voices eros and birth—the mental resurrection of her life and love: junebugs, berries, the birth of her children, and erotic moments with Cholly. In a reverie represented in a simulated "dialogue" with the ostensible omniscient narrative voice,[6] Pauline speaks of her losses: loss of the springtime of her youth, loss of her love for her children, and loss of the most memorable moments with her husband. Her narrative begins with part of the epigraph describing the mother, "SEEMOTHERMOTHERISVERYNICE" (88), and with two paragraphs describing her disillusion of a notion of beauty she had appropriated from the movies. This rather long description is followed by a short nostalgic paragraph in which Pauline describes the night she and her family left the South ("down home"). This pattern of narration—exteriority and interiority—continues with the narrator describing surface things, offering a bit of history, while Pauline gives us insight into her conflicted and tortured soul. Pauline's description of her erstwhile love affair and marriage permits the reader to see and hear her perspective on things she perceives to be relevant to her happiness as a wife and mother. In an unmediated voice Pauline is able, for a while at least, to win the reader's sympathy and affectively pull the reader into her psyche.[7]

Like Claudia, who reevaluates the pain of her youth and later admits that her mother's edginess was a sign of love, Pauline recalls moments of the past in order to reassure herself that the pain of the present has not always been there. Unlike Claudia's reevaluation of her parents' love ("So when I think of autumn, I think of somebody with hands who does not want me to die" [14]), Pauline's recollections of the joys of her youth are momentary escapes from the pain of the present. And contrary to Aunt Jimmy and the visitors to her sickroom—women who have recognized and accepted the "miseries" and "joys" as part of life—for Pauline such binaries cannot exist simultaneously within one person. For her, one is either happy or sad, suffering or living a life of eternal springtime bliss. As a result, she becomes the author of her own narrative of self-hatred, child abuse, and marital violence—somatic expressions of internal pressures prompted by external events. Pauline, especially in agonized musings, laments what were once for her the supreme pleasures of nature and human companionship. Her reveries of the joys of childhood and young adulthood ironically reinforce her pain because they belong to an irrevocable past. As a child, she had "cultivated quiet and private pleasures" (88). Her penchant for order meant that "whatever portable plurality she found, she organized into neat lines, according to their size, shape, or gradations of color" (89), as though by ordering the spaces she inhabited she might deflect attention from her deformed foot.

Pauline's recollections of happier times center on her marriage, which has been "shredded by quarrels" (94). Yet she contends that "it wasn't all bad" (102). For two pages she describes erotic moments with Cholly, which she associates with the internalized colors of her youth: *"I begin to feel those little bits of color floating up into me—deep in me. That streak of green from the june-bug light, the purple from the berries trickling along my thighs. Mama's lemonade yellow runs sweet in me. Then I feel like I'm laughing between my legs, and the laughing gets mixed up with the colors, and I'm afraid I'll come, and afraid I won't. But I know I will"* (103–4). To her employer's question about Cholly's neglect of his spousal duties as a husband—*"What good is he, Pauline, what good is he to you?"*—Pauline responds with words that belie her feelings: *"No good, ma'am."* Yet she recalls that *"When I got outside, I felt the pains in my crotch, I had held my legs together so tight trying to make that woman understand"* (96). The somatic expression of her internal feelings, the*"pains in [her] crotch"* (96), is a reminder of how "good" Cholly was in bed. Elliott Butler-Evans contends that this scene depicts "one of the major areas of conflict between Black women and White women" since Pauline is compelled by "racial solidarity" to stay with Cholly and "tolerate his abuse" while she is economically dependent upon her white employer (75). I find this reading unsatisfactory because it ignores the erotic and nostalgic dimensions of Pauline's physical gesture.[8] Pauline recollects good times as well as bad, even though she realizes that *"it ain't like that no more"* and that the "only thing I miss sometimes is the rainbow"(104), a metonymy for her lost joys and lost hopes.

Pauline's narrative of losses discloses the intricacies of her story. The interweaving of former pleasures with present marital and maternal problems renders her story all the more compelling because it presents her as a woman caught in a web of contradictions comprising hatred for her husband and children and idealization of the white families who employ her. For all her access to white homes and the movies, Pauline cannot recuperate her losses in the white world. To compensate for such losses, she turns to Christianity: *"My Maker will take care of me. I know He will. I know He will."* The repetition is Pauline's call for a transcendent Providence who will make up for the lost pleasures of *"this old world"* since *"there is sure to be a glory"* (104), a prayer that finds some resonance in her daughter's belief that, through prayer, she may get blue eyes and escape the pains of this world. The narrative critiques Pauline's collusion in the destruction of her family by her failure to assume partial responsibility and accountability for her dysfunctional marriage and socially maladjusted children.

As Pauline turns to God for comfort in her isolation from Cholly and community, her daughter turns from God toward earthly, practicable solutions to her loneliness. Pecola is most often depicted as a victim and as an object of other characters' insults and violence or as an individual worthy of the reader's pity. Her subjectivity is shadowed by the emphasis on the perception of her as a victimized "other" within the African American racial and social economy. As the narrative makes abundantly clear, Pecola is overburdened by parental neglect and abuse, peer cruelty, and communal scapegoating, but what is often overlooked are Pecola's desperate, single-handed attempts to change other people's perceptions of her. Although she is impelled by a misguided notion that she, as a despised child, is responsible for her parents' violent behavior, a number of scenes reveal Pecola's self-conscious and direct attempts to change her position from that of an objectified other to that of a subject and an agent as she searches for a replacement for the tortured self she has learned to associate with her blackness. In scrutinizing Pecola as scapegoat, it is important to consider her actions as survival techniques and not merely as self-loathing or only as a desire to *be* like Shirley Temple or Mary Jane. More important, when we shift our focus from Pecola's victimization to her gestures at agency and human connectedness, we may be less inclined to pity her and more inclined to admire her. When we consider the fact that she *alone* tries to remedy her situation, and when we focus on her awareness that others see her blackness as a "curse" and on her attempts to exorcize that "curse," we may come away with a deeper understanding of her efforts to alter her appearance and her desire to make life better for herself and for her parents.

Direct access to Pecola's thoughts sans Claudia's or the narrator's influence allows readers to explore Pecola's inner world. This direct access to Pecola's thoughts is an opportunity to scrutinize Pecola's choices based on her own perception of her alienation and her lone struggles to save herself. As a ten- and an eleven-year-old isolate, Pecola decides to take her fate into her own hands. Single-handedly, she tries to alter the conditions under which she is forced to live. Although her desire for blue eyes may be the most radical expression of her determination to make life better for herself, it too frequently overshadows her other attempts to escape loneliness. "I was so lonely for friends" (152), she confides to the friend created in her psychotic mind.

One of the most revealing moments occurs early in the novel when Pecola confronts her image in the mirror, a speculum of the multiple images of her short, tortured life. This moment marks a complex contemplation of identity in that the mirror refracts the multiple self-images Pecola has internalized through the lenses of others.[9] Thus, "she would never know her beauty" and "would only see what was there to see: the eyes of other people" (40).[10] Pecola's refracted image of herself as an ugly and despised child is not unlike the image of her mother, Pauline, absorbing "self-contempt by the heap" (97) from the movie screen. Consider the following scenario:

> As long as she looked the way she did, as long as she was ugly, she would have to stay with these people. Somehow she belonged to them. Long hours she sat looking in the mirror, trying to discover the secret of ugliness, the ugliness that made her ignored or despised at school, by teach-

ers and classmates alike. She was the only member of her class who sat alone at a double desk. The first letter of her last name forced her to sit in the front of the room always. . . . Her teachers had always treated her this way. They tried never to glance at her, and called on her only when everyone was required to respond. (39–40)

These images arc back to earlier times:

> It had occurred to Pecola some time ago that if her eyes, those eyes that held the pictures, and knew the sights—if those eyes of hers were different, that is to say, beautiful, she herself would be different. Her teeth were good, and at least her nose was not big and flat like some of those who were thought so cute. If she looked different, beautiful, maybe Cholly would be different, and Mrs. Breedlove too. Maybe they'd say, "Why, look at pretty-eyed Pecola. We mustn't do bad things in front of her pretty eyes." (40)

Pecola moves from wishes to prayers: "Each night, without fail, she prayed for blue eyes. Fervently, for a year she had prayed. Although somewhat discouraged, she was not without hope. To have something as wonderful as that happen would take a long, long time" (40). Her mother's initial and prevailing negative attitude toward her—"*Lord she was ugly*" (100), her description of Pecola at birth; and later when Pecola accidentally spills the hot cobbler in the Fisher home, her mother gives her "the back of her hand" and calls her a "crazy fool" as she turns to comfort the white child, "Hush baby, hush" (86–87)—marks the beginning of Pecola's negative self-concept. The rejection of her own child for the white child, Philip Weinstein points out, is a sign of Pauline's "fatal dysfunction," which contributes to Pecola's "descent into insanity" (20). But the worst image of herself comes to Pecola from her father, who rapes her twice, and from her mother, who denies her daughter's claims about the rape—"She didn't even believe me when I told her"—prompting Pecola not to tell her about the second rape because "she wouldn't have believed me then either" (155).

Mrs. MacTeer, despite her kind concern when she discovers Pecola's menarche, is also guilty of objectifying Pecola, who, for her, is just another welfare "case" (17), some "folks," or "*any*body" (22), an additional strain on the MacTeer budget: "I got about as much business with another mouth to feed as a cat with side pockets" (23). Mrs. MacTeer's insults, although indirect and not limited to Pecola, are nevertheless "extremely painful in their thrust" (23). A child with Pecola's insecurity and sensitivity will most surely internalize such insults. It is clear that Mrs. MacTeer has some concern for Pecola's plight beyond the extra money she may gain for taking her in since she tells Claudia and Frieda "to be nice to her and not fight" (17). And while this woman's compassion for Pecola may be read in her "sorry" eyes and heard in "the music of [her] laughter" as she initiates Pecola into womanhood, their bonding is temporary, and, like Pecola's encounters with the prostitutes, it is one-sided in that the women do not show any awareness of Pecola's more pressing need. When China asks Pecola why she is not wearing socks, the issue doesn't go beyond China's playful response, "Must be somethin' in your house that loves socks" (44).

Other adults share responsibility for Pecola's psychic tension about who she is. Mr. Yacobowski's "suspended" gaze into a "vacuum" conveys to Pecola "something she has seen . . . lurking in the eyes of all white people," a "distaste for her, for her blackness," and a "total absence of human recognition" (42). Pecola sees herself erased in Yacobowski's vacant eyes and seeks solace and transformation in the Mary Jane candies she purchases from him. Yacobowski may represent the adult white gaze, but it is Geraldine and Soaphead Church who, besides Pecola's parents—especially her father who raped her—exacerbate her pathological condition. Soaphead, like Geraldine, is struggling with blackness and finds Pecola an easy target for his own self-loathing. The "ugly little girl asking for beauty" evokes Soaphead's "love and understanding," even his anger at his "powerless[ness] to help her" (137). But neither his powerlessness nor his understanding prevent him from perpetrating a fraud upon her. As the narrator observes, he is more concerned with his "mortality" that interferes with his ability to change the color of Pecola's eyes than he is with the wisdom of his decision to convince Pecola that he has indeed changed the color of her eyes (135–36).

Pecola's contemplation of her "ugliness" projects a multiple-consciousness. Denise Heinze has argued that Pecola's image of herself is refracted through a "decidedly male point of view, a Lacanian Gaze in which the appropriating gaze of the subject is male and the object of the gaze is female" (25). Heinze is partially correct in that we see several males objectifying Pecola. Such a limited gaze fails to account for other gazes such as Geraldine's and the teachers' that suggest decidedly racist attitudes. Michael Awkward comes closer to Morrison's project when he speaks of her characters' "hopelessly divided selves, selves which attempt an erasure of blackness" (*Inspiring* 80). What Pecola discerns from the mirror is a self fractured by these varied gazes. The fights between her parents fuse these images and mobilize her desire for blue eyes, not so much by her own conviction that she is ugly, but by the projection of her self through the eyes of others. How does a young girl, in the process of developing an identity and formulating a self, best see and know herself except through socialization and interaction with others? If, as she observes, children with more pronounced negroid features than hers—flatter noses and bad teeth—are considered "cute," then the fault must be in her own eyes. In other words, the contempt others have directed toward her has transmuted to self-contempt. Thus, in the absence of parental and communal nurturing and without a realistic, wholesome sense of self, Pecola searches for a suitable replacement for the rejected self she perceives as her own.

Pecola begins with wishes and prayers, and when these prove fruitless, she seeks other solutions. I want to emphasize Pecola's conscious and unwavering attempts at refashioning a self that, in her own mind, at least, comports with the one she believes others will befriend and love. Readers' outrage at the morally reprehensible behavior of Pecola's family and community toward her may blind them to Pecola's gestures at mitigating the wrongs she endures. The images of whiteness that bombard her psyche and the insults she sustains because she is black are most certainly behind her question, "How do you get someone to love you?" (29). Pecola is clearly seeking love through relationships, and her fixations on the Shirley Temple cup, the Mary Jane candies, and Geraldine's cat are overt manifestations of the internal pain she experiences as a despised black child. In accepting Maureen's invitation for ice cream and Junior's invitation to see his cat, Pecola is not just responding to coercion; she is responding to her inner loneliness and desire for companionship. Her visits with the prostitutes are self-initiated and also suggest an element of personal choice. Even her decision to seek help from Soaphead Church— "Maybe *you* can do it for me" (emphasis added)—must be read in the context of her efforts to find a solution to the hatred heaped on her: "I can't go to school no more. And I thought maybe you could help me" (137). This is the expression of an individual seeking control of her destiny by trying to counter her tortured existence.

Marta Caminero-Santangelo contends that Morrison has depicted Pecola's madness as her "inability to construct a counternarrative of any sort" (132). I would argue to the contrary: I read Pecola's dialogue with her self as a counternarrative to the narratives that have been foisted on her by others. Her questions concerning the depth of color in her eyes signal both madness and counterintuitiveness—her attempt to create order out of her chaotic world and tortured mind. I also want to resist John N. Duvall's reading of Pecola's psychic deterioration as "acquiesce[nce] to her marginalization (in a fashion that is marked as a form of unconscious complicity)" (55). The narrative suggests otherwise. Pecola's refusal to be stigmatized (even though we are inclined to judge her efforts to counter this stigmatization as socially and ethically repugnant) is her unsuccessful effort to achieve some form of human attachment as a hedge against the cruelties foisted on her. If we read her narrative as a subtext of desire and subversion, a resistance to those who have objectified her and a desire to become the beloved blue-eyed child her community privileges and adores, we can then grant her the humanity she so desperately craves.

Pecola manifests what I am calling agency in other ways. In asking Claudia, "Is it true that I can have a baby now?" Pecola exposes her desire to satisfy that desire. The question also reveals her efforts to manipulate the terms of her existence. "How do you *do* that? I mean how do you *get* somebody to love you?" (29; emphasis added), she pleads. This question suggests more than mere curiosity; her choice of verbs implies a willingness to act—to *do* whatever it takes to be loved. The ultimate tragedy for Pecola is that Claudia, like so many others in the community, fails to recognize Pecola's deepest need. Although the prostitutes may offer Pecola some "balm to soothe her psychic wounds" (Heinze 78), they are too self-absorbed to probe any further than to ask why she couldn't find any socks or to recognize that behind her question, "How come you got so many boyfriends, Miss Marie?" (44), is a deep longing for some direction in her quest for companionship. Yet those who could and should understand Pecola's desire for connection are actually those who turn from her, as the ten-year-old Claudia does when Pecola prods her for the answer. Claudia does not know the answer and, as she points out, "Frieda was asleep" (29); that is, the older more knowledgeable person was unavailable. Over the course of the novel, Pecola's question is never satisfactorily answered: What if, she wonders, "there is somebody way off somewhere with eyes bluer than mine?" (157). Pecola's pain does not sensitize Claudia or anyone else to her plight; rather, it "antagonize[s]" Claudia (61). Pecola's pain also contrasts her vulnerability to communal insults with Claudia's ability to fight for herself and her impatience with someone as weak as Pecola. Claudia "wanted to open her up, crisp her edges, ram a stick down the hunched and curving spine, force her to stand erect and spit the misery out on the street" (61). Even so, Claudia never confronts Pecola with her antagonism; she merely fights for her when the other children (Maureen, Rosemary, Bay Boy) are cruel and shares with the reader her anger at Mrs. Breedlove's neglect and cruelty. The implication is that Claudia's efforts on Pecola's behalf reveal more about Claudia's temperament than they do about her ability to assist Pecola in her search for love. But Claudia cannot comprehend Pecola's somatic symptoms of her psychic pain. It is even more doubtful whether Claudia, at age ten, would really understand, even if Pecola could verbalize such pain; after all, Claudia does not fully comprehend the source of Pecola's struggle until she is much older and Pecola has mentally deteriorated. "The most pain can do," Kristin Boudreau asserts, "is call attention to the violent and necessary process whereby self is constructed by others" (464). And the self that others see is the self that Pecola wishes to remake.[11]

Pecola's ultimate loss of self—her dissociation and isolation—is prefigured by Auntie Julia, who, according to one of Mrs. MacTeer's friends, "is trotting down Sixteenth Street talking to herself" (15). One of the women suggests that Auntie Julia should have been "confined" to an asylum for the mentally ill, but the county refused to "put [her] away" because "she wasn't harming anybody" (15). Another woman retorts, "Well, she's harming me. You want *something* to scare the living shit out of you, you get up at five-thirty in the morning like I do and see that old hag floating by in that bonnet" (15). Pecola and her unborn child are similarly mocked and objectified: "She be lucky if *it* don't live. Bound to be the ugliest *thing* walking." One woman in the community replies: "Can't help but be. Ought to be a law: two ugly people doubling up like that to make more *ugly*" (148; emphasis added). This echolalia of the narrator's description of the Breedloves' conviction that they are "ugly" becomes a part of the community's prevailing view of them. This conviction becomes lodged in Pecola's psyche. Her question, "How do you get someone to love you?" is a pivotal moment in her narrative because it comes long before her psychic disintegration. It also presages her physical rape by her father and psychological rape by Soaphead Church. Claudia's answer, "I didn't know," contrasts the relationships within the Breedlove and the MacTeer households. Claudia doesn't know because love has never been an issue for her; her parents and sister, through their actions, reveal their love for her. Pecola, on the other hand, purchases Mary Jane candy—a substitution for familial and communal love: "Three pennies had bought nine lovely orgasms with Mary Jane. Mary Jane, for whom a candy was named" (43). As an adult, Claudia assesses the physical and psychic effects of the various assaults on Pecola, but she belatedly recognizes the community's complicity: "We honed our ego on her, our characters with her frailty, and yawned in the fantasy of our strength" (159). When we last see her, she is emotionally and psychically mangled:[12] "The damage done [to Pecola] was total" (159).

Morrison's move from *The Bluest Eye* to *Song of Solomon* marks a shift in narrative structure and in narrated suffering. In the former she gives us direct access to Pecola's and Pauline's interior lives, while in the latter she narrates Pilate's interior spaces through an omniscient voice. We can also discern Pilate's feelings through her songs and direct speech. Pilate's song at the opening of the novel is a dirge for Mr. Robert Smith and a lament for the loss of several important men in her life—her father by murder; her brother to money, ambition, and class consciousness; and her actual or potential husbands because of her missing navel. Marilyn Sanders Mobley observes that Pilate's "voice not only disrupts the gaze of the crowd at the spectacle of Mr. Smith . . . but also introduces her as an alternate narrative voice, whose story in song prompts the crowd to listen to her." Mobley rightly notes that at this point in the novel Pilate's song is "disruptive," and that its words "clarify" nothing for the audience or reader. Mobley further observes that "the sniggering response of some and the silent listening of others suggest the crowd's acceptance of Pilate's voice and presence" ("Call" 51). We witness a similar call and response at Hagar's funeral when Pilate and Reba stir the congregation with their dirge on "mercy." Pilate's vocal variations on "mercy"—statement and question—from a "shouted" "I want mercy" to a "clear bluebell voice" are answered by Reba's "sweet soprano," "I hear you," and by those in the congregation "who had the nerve to look at her, shake their heads, and say, 'Amen'" (317–18). The rise and fall of Pilate's voice and its variations register the depths of Pilate's grief for the death of her granddaughter and for her self-enforced isolation from a community whose "glance would climb no higher than the long black fingers at her side" (319). Barbara Hill Rigney describes Pilate's "howl" (319) at Hagar's funeral as a "universal loss, a cry for 'Mercy!' that resonates from the unconscious, from the 'jungle' part of Pilate's mind" (20).[13] The narrator's depiction of this scene—in the discourse of the "jungle"—does not suggest the jungle in Pilate. Rather it insists on the primal responses death evokes. The discourse is metaphorical: "Suddenly, *like* [emphasis added] an elephant who has just found his anger and lifts his trunk over the heads of the little men who want his teeth or his hide or his flesh or his amazing strength, Pilate trumpeted for the sky itself to hear, 'And she was *loved*!'" (319). Pilate's eulogy combines threat—"I'll find who's botherin my sweet sugar lumpkin. / I'll find who's botherin my baby" (318)—and promise. Her aside to the congregation that Hagar "was *loved*!" is an assertion about the caring atmosphere in their home and a lament for Pilate's forced isolation. Wendy Harding and Jacky Martin locate Pilate's isolation in an "alterity" that "allows her to invent herself" (72).

Pilate's song at Mr. Smith's suicide—itself a modification of a song from her childhood—later, with further modification by Milkman, serves as her own dirge. "Sing a little somethin for me," she implores Milkman, who obliges:

> Sugargirl don't leave me here
> Cotton balls to choke me
> Sugargirl don't leave me here
> Buckra's arms to yoke me. (336)

The ostensible symmetry in the novel—the beginning, a suicide, and the end, a murder—is subtly deceptive. Pilate's song at the scene of Mr. Smith's suicide is a response to the immediacy of the moment and the pain it evokes. Her request to Milkman to "sing a little somethin *for me*" is her request for something for herself. Even her dying words—"I wish I'd a knowed more people. I would of loved 'em all. If I'd a knowed more, I would a loved more" (336; emphasis added)—may sound "sweet" and self-serving. But these words are, in fact, a coda to the contradictions of life that balance generosity and alienation and establish possibilities for understanding and compassion emanating from alienation. Duvall interprets Pilate's remarks as her "ability to transcend self and self-love" (96). Rather than transcending self-love, Pilate's statement evinces her ability to love both herself and others, in the face of their refusal to accept and love her. Pilate's love of self and others, Morrison observes, derives from the fact that Pilate had had "a dozen years of a nurturing relationship with . . . a father, and she had a brother who loved her very much, and she could use that knowledge of that love for her life" (McKay, "Interview" 419).

Pilate informs Ruth that during the three years in New York, where she worked among migrants, they "treated me fine," and "I didn't have a thought in my head of ever leavin them." Yet she "had to, [because] after a while they didn't want me around no more. . . . On account of my stomach?" she inquires. The answer she gets is silence and heads turned toward the ground (142–44). The narrator recounts most of Pilate's history, often interpreting it with Pilate's language. Why does Morrison use a mediated voice for this discourse between Pilate and the reader? Perhaps Morrison wants to restrain Pilate for fear of her taking over what is designated as a male-centered narrative. In the scenes where Pilate sings her repressed grief, she disrupts the silence and momentarily possesses the scenes in question—the suicide scene, Hagar's funeral, and her own death scene. But why else would Morrison choose an intervening voice for a simulated dialogue between Pilate and the reader? Can it be that Pilate's compassion for others might cloud her vision and cause her to think less of her own suffering than of the actions of those who contributed to it? Can it be that Pilate, at the level of "high ignorance," can neither fully appreciate nor express the depth of her rejection occasioned by her difference? Perhaps only an omniscient voice can recite Pilate's history of isolation and internal suffering with its nuances and subtleties that render her story a larger commentary on the communities she inhabits. In other words, Pilate's deep capacity for love and generosity is exceeded only by the community's rejection based on her physical difference alone. But those who see her smooth stomach question her humanity: "What are you? Some kinda *mer*maid?" (148). The re-creation of Pilate's compassion and generosity is the answer to that question.

Perhaps Pilate's most poignant "song" is her song of resignation and response to her condition as "other." Unlike Pauline Breedlove, who sees herself as different from the women in Lorain and unable to bond with them despite her efforts at imitating their dress and trying to improve her speech, and Pecola, who sets out to change the community's perception of her, Pilate studies her situation, then decides to create her own happiness based on her own measured values. Morrison uses an unidentified narrator to analyze Pilate's pain, no doubt because Pilate may lack the appropriate language to describe her innermost thoughts. I do not mean to suggest that Pilate's feelings or desires are less poignant than the narrator's. Rather, the narrator reflects Pilate's hesitation to state her desires and the necessity for a voice commensurate with Pilate's situation and thwarted desires. Elaine Scarry's theory of pain is relevant here (though she is concerned with physical pain on a larger scale, pain engendered by famine, war, etc.). Scarry writes, "Because the person in pain is ordinarily bereft of the language resources of speech, it is not surprising that the language for pain should sometimes be brought into being by those who are not themselves in pain but who speak on behalf of those who are." Scarry observes that "psychological suffering, though often difficult to express, *does* have referential context, *is* susceptible to verbal objectification, and so . . . is habitually depicted in art" (*Body* 6, 11). In Pilate's case, it is the narrator who summarizes Pilate's situation—"She [begins] at zero"—and raises the fundamental questions: "When am I happy and when am I sad and what is the difference? What do I need to know to stay alive? What is true in this world?" These are large questions for a woman "hampered by huge ignorances." The narrator hastens to add that ignorance is not the antithesis of intelligence, that Pilate is "not in any way unintelligent." Her mind is capable of both achieving "profundity" and understanding the "revelations of a three-year-old" (149).

Pilate's isolation from the community engenders "compassion for troubled people" and keeps "her just barely within the boundaries of the elaborately socialized world of black people" (149). This statement exposes the difficulty a person like Pilate faces in trying to negotiate a comfortable place within the black community in particular and within society at large. Pilate's alienation, therefore, economically and socially marginalizes her. Pilate's condition also reveals the psychological and economic distance between herself and her brother, Macon, by contrasting the self-generated pleasures and unity within Pilate's household with the loneliness and sterility that characterize her brother's. The harmonious blending of the women's voices in Pilate's house is set in opposition to the strident, often silenced voices of the three women in her brother's house, where he "kept each member of his family awkward with fear" (10). Macon is softened, if only briefly, by the sounds of their voices: "the irritability of the day drain[s] from him" as he "relishe[s] the effortless beauty of the women singing in the candlelight" (29). Their music, a maieutic, temporarily enables him to reconnect with his past and his cultural heritage.[14]

Song of Solomon is also a song of dispossession and repossession. Pilate's losses—her father, her brother, her granddaughter, and her community—become Milkman's gains as he develops the capacity to love. Pilate's song of longing and generosity, together with Macon's song of greed, bequeaths to Milkman a song of knowledge and responsibility. What Milkman learns in Danville, Pennsylvania, and Shalimar, Virginia, is not just a history of his ancestors but the depth of his Aunt Pilate's love, which reaches even into her willingness to accept the fatal bullet intended for him.

If Pilate's narrative is an expression of maternal love and indulgence, in *Beloved* Sethe's narrative is, by contrast, a plea for a mother's right to love her own—an insistence upon the natural law of maternal love and an account of the pain prompted by the loss of maternal agency. What differentiates this maternal pain? The fundamental difference lies in the way Sethe and her children are treated in contradistinction to the way white families and free black families are treated. Sethe and her children are denied the fundamental human rights of freedom and familial bonds. They are by law chattel—they can be sold, traded, and bartered like animals.

Hortense Spillers's analysis of gender as it relates to African Americans provides a background for Sethe's maternal suffering. In "Mama's Baby," Spillers argues that the traditional categories of gender lose their integrity when one seeks to apply them to the African American cultural community because such gender categories are constrained by the subject position of African Americans at the moment of rupture in Black

African culture, beginning with the Atlantic slave trade and its effects. In this essay, Spillers reminds us that the subject positions of the African American female must be traced back to the moment of enslavement, when black women were simultaneously granted and denied motherhood. This designation of "motherhood" to the slave is a misnomer and certainly a vexed term, since a slave did not legally own her children: both she and they were properties of the slaveholder. While the laws of slavery ordained that the child's condition followed the mother's, economic concerns most often dictated whether or not a child remained with a parent. In *Beloved*, several women inscribe their maternal narratives against the patriarchal discourse within the slave system.

For a slave mother to assert ownership of her children was to deny the slaveholder the same right. This opposition between the slave's maternal rights and the slaveholder's legal claims upon slave children was frequently played out in the marketplace when slaveholders sought to separate mothers from their children. The legal claims by the slaveholder over the natural rights of the mother meant that the mother-child relationship had to be disallowed. Many slave mothers were reluctant to bring children into a world where their future was already determined. Yet the very system that sought to negate black motherhood created the possibilities for the subversion of the slaveholders' authority. The efforts of slave women to assert their rights as mothers prove that, in defiance of the slaveholders' power, they were insisting that maternity was not in the slaveholders' hands but in the physical and affective bonds between mothers and their children. In *Beloved*, Morrison asks, What happens when a slave mother directly challenges such a system by insisting on her right to "own" the children she has borne, regardless of the man or men who fathered them? The text explores this opposition between the mother's natural rights and the slaveholder's legal and economic claims by configuring the agonizing memories of slave women's maternal experiences. Several women are deeply scarred as maternal figures: some have taken drastic measures to thwart the master's control; others have quietly endured their pain; still others have chosen denial. When Ella meets Sethe and her day-old child, Ella admonishes Sethe, "Don't love nothing" (92). But Sethe's fate has been different from Ella's; Sethe has had the rare, though not unique, distinction of being married to one man and bearing four children within that union. This fact more than any other, perhaps, accounts for Sethe's insistence upon her maternal rights.

Sethe's claims of ownership of her children challenge Garner's ostensibly benign system of servitude, in which he boasts of treating his slaves as "men." Garner's "model" plantation, contrary to his expectation of producing contented slaves, throws the horror of that system into harsh relief by depicting men resorting to sodomy in the absence of women and a son forced to work five years of Sundays to purchase his lame mother's freedom, even though she has rendered fifty years of unremunerated service. Baby Suggs represents the slave woman who has given birth to numerous children and watched as they were snatched from her one by one. "I had eight," she says. "Every one of them gone away from me. Four taken, four chased, and all, I expect, worrying somebody's house into evil. My first-born. All I can remember of her is how she loved the burned bottom of bread." She asks, "Can you beat that? Eight children and that's all I remember" (5). Her statement reminds us that slave mothers memorized identifying marks and other features of their offspring in hopes of recognizing them in the future:[15] "Seven times [Baby Suggs] had . . . held a little foot; examined the fat fingertips with her own—fingers she never saw become the male or female hands a mother would recognize anywhere" (139). Baby Suggs's maternal narrative recounts the dilemma of mothers snared by a system that could, at a whim or the stroke of a pen, deny human feelings and sever family bonds. Baby Suggs's reverie underscores the poignancy of her narrative by calling the reader's attention to the power of blood and maternal bonds; the "fact was she knew more about them than she knew about herself, having never had the map to discover what she was like" (140). Her attempts to harden herself against the inevitable, yet somehow clinging to bits of memories of her children, belie the notion that slave women showed a callous disregard for their children—Ella's "Don't love nothing" notwithstanding. In a society where the demands of the slaveholder nearly always infringed upon the slave mother's loyalty to her own, she had to sequester her love for her children in the crowded slave quarters and in the privacy of her mind.

Within this system that denied slaves their subjectivity, Sethe emerges as a complex, subversive character who refuses to submit to a practice designed to undermine all feelings and negate the very foundation of motherhood. Sethe's relationship with her own children differs significantly from Baby Suggs's. First of all, as Baby Suggs reminds us, Sethe has had the "amazing luck of six whole years of marriage" to one man who "fathered every one of her children" (23). Behind Baby Suggs's reminder is the memory of the brutal system in which she was raped by several white men and the knowledge that only her son Halle, Sethe's husband, had a black father. The use of Baby Suggs as a sexually abused and an embittered woman is a reminder, as Darlene Clark Hine rightly states, that, while "it would be a mistake to see black women solely as victims under slavery," it would also be a mistake "to create myths of the superheroic black woman who stoically met every obstacle, endured total debasement, only to rise above her captors" (341). Ella's "If anybody was to ask me I'd say, 'Don't love nothing'" (92), is an ostensible stoicism borne of Ella's imprisonment by "two men—a father and son," who "kept her locked in a room for themselves" (119).

Unlike Ella and Baby Suggs, Sethe has found ways to maintain a close physical relationship with her children for two important reasons: the level of "respect" Garner has accorded the slaves on his farm and Sethe's fierce attachment to her children. She is outraged at the unfairness of a system in which "little white babies got [her mother's milk] first and I got what was left or none" (200). Equating milk with motherhood and the physical connection between mother and child, Sethe is horrified by the notion that someone else could preempt her children's claim to their birthright. "Nobody will ever get my milk no more except my children" (200), she vows. Her language is defiant and potentially subversive; it anticipates her decision to disempower her master and her children's presumptive owner. The defiant tone presages the traumatic decision she makes twenty-eight days after her escape to freedom. The notion of owning her self—body and offspring—drives her to infanticide. Caminero-Santangelo has noted that "madness in all of Morrison's fiction is consistently linked with destructive impulses directed inward, which thus become another aspect of the already oppressive situation of racism" (137). *Beloved* graphically depicts the emotional trauma slave women endured after forced separation from their children, such as Baby Suggs's recognition that "nobody stopped playing checkers just because the pieces included her children" (23). And, despite Baby Suggs's contention that "it was not worth the trouble to learn features you would never see change into adulthood" (139), the agony of not seeing seven of them grow into adulthood haunts her until her death.

Sethe's narrative counters and reinforces the other maternal narratives by the force of her conviction not to surrender, regardless of the cost to herself and the children. Her defiance trumps the master narrative of ownership because she is willing to make the ultimate sacrifice on her own terms: if her children are to be taken from her, she will be the agent of their removal. Such defiance further reveals Sethe's desire to achieve subjectivity for herself and her children by assuming responsibility for their fate. Her children exist for her on a human level, and she responds to them with unbridled maternal love, their enslaved condition notwithstanding. In an apostrophe to her murdered child, Sethe describes an

Edenic site where her children played freely before schoolteacher came to manage the Garner farm. She watched them even while she worked in the fields. She tells the absent Beloved, "I put my hoe down and cut across the side yard to get to you. . . . I wanted to pick you up in my arms and look at you sleeping too. Didn't know which; you had the sweetest face" (192). The poignancy of maternal memory in this passage and Baby Suggs's recollections of her lost children reveal the traumatic choices open to enslaved mothers—bitter acceptance and submission or open defiance. Whatever the choice, the pain of separation remained.

Sethe, the doting mother, is soon transformed into "la mère sauvage" or the altruistic mother, depending on how we interpret her actions, though in her own mind, she is acting as the altruistic mother, "trying to outhurt the hurter" (234). In her revulsion at schoolteacher's use of her body, she acts out a rebellion against his racist theory and objectifying practice: "They handled me like I was the cow" (200). At that moment she vows that "no one, nobody on this earth, would list her daughter's characteristics on the animal side of the paper" (251). So when schoolteacher comes to Cincinnati to reclaim her and her children, Sethe thwarts him by murdering one of her children and severely injuring the others. In this violent display of love, she asserts her maternal autonomy in order to save her children from what she believes is a condition worse than death. But even she is frightened by her passionate claims, because she knows that, "unless carefree, motherlove was a killer" (132)—a message she has finally learned from Baby Suggs and Ella. Morrison terms Sethe's commitment to her children "an excess of maternal feeling, a total surrender" (Darling 9). Such a surrender is figured in Sethe's desire to protect her children from the atrocities she endured in slavery. Confronted with the ultimate reality of the slaveholder's power, however, Sethe resorts to infanticide. In challenging a system that sought to deny her maternal access to her children, Sethe stubbornly refuses to abdicate her maternal role, and in doing so she not only achieves that role but emerges as a full human being—though scarred and confused.

If the pain of thwarted maternal love leads to infanticide in *Beloved*, in *Jazz* the failure of maternity and its concomitant aches contribute, in part, to Violet Trace's violence. Violet's pain is represented as a psychosis overtly manifested in her mutilation of the corpse of her husband's young mistress and her theft of a neighbor's child, engendered, perhaps, by years of repressed desire and a haunting fear of abandonment and loneliness. The intrusive narrative voice steps aside and permits the narrative of Violet's struggles with psychic tensions to unfold in three distinct ways. One method is a series of conversations between Violet and Alice in which Violet speaks about her mental suffering while Alice draws her out with a question, a comment, or advice. The second method entails the exposure of Alice's true feelings through her unspoken thoughts. The third method involves Felice's long interior monologue in which she fills in information about Dorcas's murder and apprises the reader of the progress of Joe and Violet's reconciliation. These strategies disrupt the narrator's telling through a series of mental flashbacks in which each of the three women muses on her past. These musings are filtered through the narrative voice that appropriates Violet's and Alice's discourses but permits Felice's thoughts to flow uninterrupted. The open dialogues—observed and reported—function as a patient-psychiatrist encounter, where the "patient" (Violet) discusses the strain in her "head" and the "psychiatrist" (Alice or Felice) listens but says very little, while the reader takes on the role of voyeur. The narrative voice moves in and out, speculating and interpreting yet recognizing the value of the characters' own voices and thoughts.

The loss of three unborn children and the pain of her husband's infidelity exact their toll. To counter the conscious decision not to have children and to repress the unconscious desire to have them, Violet removes a neighborhood child from its carriage and takes it home, and she hides a doll under her bed, imagining it as one of her lost fetuses: "The memory of the light, however, that had skipped through her veins" when she held the stolen child "came back now and then," and "she imagined a brightness that could be carried in her arms" (22). Eventually, she is forced to confront her prolonged displaced desires—her caged birds and the parrot she taught to say, "I love you." Violet's conversation with her birds is analogous to Pecola's dialogue with the imaginary friend. Pain, anger, and aberrant behavior lead to her husband's silence and abandonment once he realizes that "he is married to a woman who speaks mainly to her birds" (24). The caged birds are a problematic symbol of projection and control. If we read them as figures of the unborn fetuses who might have come to term, would they have been Violet's trap to prevent Joe's infidelity? Or had she brought these fetuses to term, would they have changed Joe's attitude about fatherhood? On one level these birds may be Violet's reenactment of her mother's loneliness and suicide, a type of matrophobia, "the fear not of one's mother or of motherhood but of *becoming* one's mother" (qtd. in Rich 235).

Through the Traces' dysfunctional marriage we see the dangerous effects of unfulfilled desires. Violet mutilates Dorcas's corpse—she is "proud of trying to kill a dead girl" (94), is obsessed by a desire to know who Dorcas was and why Joe was attracted to her: "I wanted to see what kind of girl he'd rather me be" (82), and is determined to learn all she can about her rival—where she went for entertainment; how she styled her hair; how she dressed—anything to explain Joe's love for the girl. As if to remind herself of her failures as a spouse, Violet keeps a photograph of Dorcas in full view. On the day she cuts the throat of her murdered rival, Violet releases her birds "to freeze or fly" (3). In freeing them she recognizes their surrogacy for Joe and her unborn children. Freeing the birds likewise represents her first steps toward confronting her fractured consciousness and her demons. The contiguity of Dorcas's funeral and the release of the birds also marks the beginning of the revival of their marriage, though not until Violet has talked through her problems with another person. Through a "stream of confidences" shared with Alice, Felice, and finally her husband, Violet finds "that Violet" who is not "Violent" (16).

One part of Violet, the intact part, knows that Alice, Felice, and others can accept physical suffering, even grief up to a point, but Violet's "crack[up]" as a maieutic for mental and emotional suffering appears, at first, beyond their ken. They may tolerate it, even joke about it, because neither Violet nor they view psychosis or neurosis as suffering; it is too abstract, too distant, and therefore beyond their understanding of human suffering.[16] But Violet's "cracks," like Pecola's psychosis, distance her from others and exacerbate her loneliness. Through their interactions with Violet, these characters recognize her mental anguish within themselves. Once Violet overcomes her obsession with Joe's dead lover, confronts her past, and accepts the reality of her marriage to Joe and the pain of her mental breakdowns, she and Joe can achieve love and intimacy. Violet's substitution of milkshakes and "Dr. Dee's Nerve and Flesh Builder" (93), like Pecola's use of milk from a Shirley Temple mug, cannot fill the empty spaces that call for human contact and love.

In *Jazz*, women's abandonment and loneliness are situated in a place where "a sorrow" sometimes "slips" in, but the characters "don't know where from" (16), at least not in the beginning. Violet is acutely aware of her mental state and wants to control or subsume it under a more acceptable and palatable name—sickness: "All my troubles be over if I could get my body sick stead of my head" (84). Violet articulates the need for an objective sign of her suffering—a scar, a physical sensation, an absence, perhaps, like Pilate's missing navel. This need to transfer her mental suffering to her body partially confirms Karl Marx's assertion that "there is only one antidote to mental suffering, and that is physical pain" (qtd. in Scarry, *Body* 33). When, during her first visit, Alice advises her to "see a doctor" for the "trouble with [her] head," Violet responds, "I just want to sit down on your chair" (80), and later adds, "I can't find a place where I can just sit down" (80–81). On her second visit, Violet explains, "I had to sit down somewhere. I thought I could do it here. That you would let me and you did" (82). Violet is aware that her psychological breakdown, or "private crack" (22), her mind's response to extreme pressure, is the root of her pain. "I'm not the one you need to be scared of," she informs Alice, implying that her aberrant behavior, the part she cannot control, is "what hurts my head" (80).

Within the context of pain is the desire to be healed and the recognition of the need for a concrete remedy: the need to sit in Alice's chair is the need for an understanding and sympathetic listener: "We born around the same time, me and you. . . . We women, me and you. Tell me something real" (110).[17] Alice, over time, becomes the kind of listener Violet needs. Although Alice never tells Violet that she herself had to share her husband with another woman, Violet "opened up" the necessity for the "kind of clarity crazy people need." Alice privately reveals her own "cracks"—thirty years of clinging to a failed marriage by using "scraps" of her dead husband's shirts as "dust cloths, monthly rags, rags tied around pipe joints to hinder freezing; pot holders and pieces to test hot irons and wrap their handles"; "wicks for oil lamps; salt bags to scrub the teeth" (83). Conversations with Violet reveal Alice's own desire—performed in language, not in deed—to kill her husband's lover and lead to her understanding of Violet's mutilation of Dorcas's corpse. When her husband, at Alice's command, chooses his lover, Alice thinks of numerous ways to attack her rival: "an ice pick stuck in and pulled up," "a clothesline rope circling her neck," mount a horse "then ride it and find the woman alone on a road and gallop till she ran her down under four iron hooves; then back again, and again until there was nothing left but tormented road dirt signaling where the hussy had been" (86). Thus when she tells Violet, "You don't know what loss is," she is speaking as much to herself because she "listened as closely to what she was saying" as Violet did (87). Alice's interior thoughts contrast with Violet's overt actions.

Felice is attracted to Violet for similar reasons. She concludes that if "Violent [*sic*] was good enough for [Alice] to let in, she was good enough for me not to be afraid of." Like Alice, Felice recognizes Violet's honesty, that "nothing she says is a lie the way it is with most older people" (205). Through Violet's honesty, Felice is mentally able to work through unresolved issues related to her mother and her ambiguous friendship with Dorcas. She understands Violet's other self—"having another you inside that isn't anything like you" (208). The "other" Felice is the one haunted by guilt associated with the ring she watched her mother steal from Tiffany's and present to Felice as a purchased gift, the same ring she had loaned Dorcas but had not recovered. By listening to Violet talk about her lost and recovered self, Felice is able to confront her true feelings about Dorcas, "How she liked to push people, men," and how Dorcas had "all those ingredients of pretty and the recipe didn't work" (206). Felice's musings on Dorcas, her mother, and Violet provide spaces for Felice's self-healing. Although she doesn't speak her thoughts to Violet and Joe, her Friday night visits give her access to their recovery and, through interior musing, effect her own recovery.

The intrusive mother figure circulates through these women-centered dialogues. Violet's conversation with Felice stirs Felice's thoughts about her own mother's failures. During one of Violet's conversations with Alice—they discuss what constitutes adult behavior—when Violet asks, "Where the grown people? Is it us?" Alice blurts out, "Oh, Mama," a vocalization of Violet's thoughts, "Mama, Mama?" (110). Their simultaneous invocation of their mothers inheres in the intimacy of the moment and in the reader's recognition that their sharing has been more than a reciprocal healing; it has been a kind of mother/daughter relationship. This moment directs us to Violet's need to sit in Alice's chair, her need *not* "to sit at the table alone in the moonlight, sipping boiled coffee . . . pretending to sip it when it was gone" (97). Violet's interior musing is followed by an apostrophe to her mother in which Violet tries to understand her own condition: "Mama? Is this where you got to and couldn't do it no more? The place of shade without trees where you know you are not and never again will be loved by anybody who can choose to do it? Where everything is over but talking?" (110). Violet's references are to her mother's silent withdrawal after the father's desertion and the repossession of their real and moveable property, including the chair her mother sat in— "stood stock-still when they tipped her from [it]" (102). Still trying to understand her condition and find some causation for her schizophrenia, Violet speaks to Felice: "Now I want to be the woman my mother didn't stay around long enough to see. That one. The one she would have liked and the one I used to like before" (208). The repeated insertions of her mother into the narrative invite reflections on both women. Will Violet repeat her mother's suicidal gesture? How much did her relationship with her mother shape the woman Violet/Violent? And what interest does the eighteen-year-old Felice have in the fifty-year-old Violet?

Violet tells Felice that she has lost a part of herself, "put her down someplace and forgot where" (211). In this dialogue, Felice, like Alice, stands in for the reader. Through her silent interest and occasional questions, Felice extracts information from Violet that gives the reader access to Violet's thoughts about her condition. Violet's need for a sympathetic listener is evidenced by her frequent visits to Alice Manfred's apartment and by her invitation to Felice to come to their home every Friday for dinner.

Violet's statement, "Everybody I grew up with is down home. We don't have children. He's what I got. He's what I got" (111), and Alice's declaration, "You don't know what loss is" (87), suggest that Violet's cure is achieved through Alice's and Felice's need for a Violet who can speak openly and honestly, her mental stresses notwithstanding. Joe's midlife crisis, infidelity with Dorcas, is equaled by Violet's belated recognition that "just when her nipples had lost their point, mother hunger had hit her like a hammer." Her "longing" for children "became heavier than sex: a panting, unmanageable craving" (108). The narrator reveals that Violet's decision to "never never have children," to never allow a "small dark foot [to] rest on another while a hungry mouth said, Mama?" (102), was made at a time when Violet watched her mother in a paralytic stupor induced by her husband's desertion—"got up and quit" (138)—for a political party that espoused voting rights for blacks. The truth is that Violet and Joe "liked children. Loved them even" (107). But, by the time they realize their mistake, they are too old to have children and so uncommunicative that each has already sought comfort outside the marriage bed—Violet with her doll and Joe with Dorcas. The mending of the broken marriage is effected through conversations with Alice, who also knows the pain occasioned by infidelity. Alice urges Violet, "Mind what's left to you. . . . I'm sayin make it, make it!" (113). The urgency of these two women's bonding over shared losses and their mutual healing is represented by the burned garment Alice is ironing. When they laugh hysterically over the fact that Alice has been so absorbed in Violet's and her own pain that she has forgotten the hot iron resting on the garment, the healing process begins. Violet remembers "that laughter is serious. More complicated, more serious than tears" (113)—a reminder to the reader that at the moment when the laughter seems to be about a burned shirt it has the complexity of True Belle's, Violet's grandmother's, laughter when she came to Virginia and looked at the tragic scene of pain and poverty that characterized her catatonic daughter's and grandchildren's lives. Laughter is the first gesture toward remedying their condition, a laughter that characterizes and propels Violet toward solving the "sickness" in her head and home.

Alice's "You got anything left to you to love, anything at all, do it" (112), in contrast to Ella's "don't love nothing," is an admonition to Violet to take whatever shards she can of her failing marriage and focus on repairing it. Concentrate on your living husband; forget your dead rival is the core of Alice's message, because she knows the agony of the refusal to accept human frailty. Felice's visits are spaced in such a way that the reader is aware that over time she and we can realistically accept the changes in Violet and Joe. This strategy helps us notice when Violet begins to follow Alice's advice, to be alert to moments when she has picked up the pieces of her marriage and worked at making it whole again. Evidence for the recuperation of their marriage comes in words and gestures: "'Thank you, baby. Take half for yourself.' Something about the way he said it. As though he appreciated it." Felice notices that "when he leaves the room and walks past his wife, he touches her. Sometimes on the head. Sometimes just a pat on her shoulder" (207). Violet's own recuperation is achieved when she has "killed the me that killed Dorcas," after she has "looked" at the two Violets—the aberrant (Violent) and the nostalgic (Violet)—and reconciled these subjectivities, yet knowing that she can never be whole.

The need for another human, someone to stand in for the absent spouse or lover or mother, a shoulder to cry on—these are the other side of Violet's hunger for wholeness. Her breakdown requires some external mediation, some intersubjective sharing. If Violet is to regain a semblance of a coherent self, she must find it in human companionship and conversation—talking is a necessary part of the cure.[18] As Gurleen Grewal observes, with Alice's help, Violet "is no longer disassociated from herself" (135).[19] Unlike Pauline and Pecola, who lack attentive and understanding friends, Violent finds such a friend in Alice Manfred. Through Violet, and coextensively through Alice and Felice, we gain a deeper understanding of psychic pain and the curative power of sharing and compassion—the power of patience and the willingness to forgive, even though one may never forget the infidelity and loss. Or, to repeat the narrator's assertion, it/Morrison has presented these broken lives to show that they can be fictionally repaired.

For Morrison, the African American usable past is situated in "rememory"[20]—a remembrance fraught with abhorrent images at times too painful and frightening to face, at other times poignant and memorable.

Violet's life, like the lives of the other women discussed in this chapter, is proof that "rememory" can surface at the slightest suggestion. Whatever their content and source, such memories are freighted with the trauma of what it means to be black and female in America. Paul Ricoeur's assertion that "suffering cries for vengeance and calls for narrative" (*Time and Narrative* 1:75) is a suitable commentary on Morrison's narratives of black women's suffering.

4 Playing with Narrative: Figuring the Reader, Refiguring History

> Pat had wanted proof in documents where possible to match the stories, and where proof was not available she interpreted—freely but, she thought, insightfully because she alone had the required emotional distance.
>
> —Toni Morrison, *Paradise*

The initial and prevailing responses (to date) to *Paradise* can be summarized in a few words—"dense," "complex," "difficult," "troubling," and "obscure." Michiko Kakutani contends that *Paradise* is "a heavy-handed, schematic piece of writing" and "a contrived, formulaic book that mechanically pits men against women" ("Worthy Women"). On the other hand, Michael Wood speaks of the "density of the novel's argument about race" and about the "complexity of its mediation on history" (114). The novel has also been praised for the "pleasures" it brings to readers familiar with Morrison's other novels.[1] I cite these divergent readings of *Paradise* as evidence that the novel opens up a plethora of interpretive moments for the patient and engaged reader. An examination of this writerly-readerly aspect of Morrison's narrative strategies will help clear up some of the denseness and seeming obscurity of *Paradise*.

Nettled by comments that *Paradise* is "'difficult' writing" and thus difficult reading, Morrison has remarked that such comments evince "different expectations" and "different yearnings . . . for black literature": the notion that certain readers may be looking for assurances that the novel will give them a comfort zone, one in which they are not expected to assume responsibility or "blame." Such a suggestion may also imply that African American literature and African American lives do not warrant and, therefore, cannot sustain the narrative enjambment that characterizes this novel. Yet in *Paradise* Morrison is "just trying to look at something without blinking," since, for her, "novels are always inquiries" (Jaffrey 7). From Morrison's inquiries into human relations vis-à-vis African Americans and patriarchal practices and from her narrative techniques we may launch a specific inquiry that privileges process over content, one that explores the relationship between the writer, the text, and the reader. This inquiry emerges from two main theoretical frames of reference: from narrative and reception theories and from a critical investigation of identity politics and gender oppression.

Paradise, like *Beloved,* engages the eras of slavery and postslavery but with a different focus; it represents a significant repetition and departure in Morrison's exploration of difference.

Paradise is about relationships complicated by race and gender, and, as in "Recitatif," the narrative is designed to confound and challenge the reader. By opening the novel with the now widely quoted sentence "They shoot the white girl first" (3)—what she calls a "throwaway"—and never identifying her, Morrison sets up the reader's expectations and prompts the reader's search for *the* "white girl."[2] Even after we complete the novel and encounter the women in their "afterlife" as escapees or resurrected figures, we still do not know which woman is white. We know, of course, that Consolata and Gigi are not white, but what about the others? It is clear from the various narratives that develop that only the white woman's racial identity is relevant in the context of the racial politics of the men who shoot her. We have seen how Morrison complicates racial identity in "Recitatif" by deflecting the question from her characters onto her readers so that the question becomes the reader's investment in race, not the characters'. In *Paradise* readers are not so much manipulated by the narrative as they are expected to manipulate the narrative in a drive toward developing readerly and writerly skills for unpacking the intratextual narratives. Unlike the unresolved question of racial identity in "Recitatif," the identity of the white woman is less important to the overarching issues in *Paradise.* Patricia's narrative is clearly a textual strategy mobilized to engage readers intimately in the narrative process.

Morrison has conceded that "by withholding racial markers from a group of black women, among whom was one white woman," she hopes to make the reader aware of "almost everything about the characters, their interior lives, their past, their faults, their strengths, except that one small piece of information which was their race." Morrison's aim is to "enforce a response in literature" whereby readers "care about," "dislike," or "dismiss the characters based on important information" other than race, and it is also "a way of saying that race is the least important piece of information about another person" ("Nobel Prize–Winning Author"). This claim by Morrison and the insertion of the sentence about the "white girl" reveal Morrison at "work" and "play," engaged in two distinct yet inseparable strategies. The former is related to the construction of narrative discourse, the latter, to reader response. Wolfgang Iser defines these strategies as "two poles": "the artistic," or "the author's text," and "the aesthetic," or "the realization accomplished by the reader" ("Interaction between Text and Reader" 106). Despite her statement of intent, Morrison is aware that once she posits "race" it will not necessarily escape the reader's mind for the duration of the narrative, whether or not she satisfies or frustrates the reader's desire to identify the raced woman. That is Morrison, the literary jester, working to catch the reader unaware and then pulling her/him in a totally different direction from the one in which the reader expects to be taken. From that point on the reader is caught in the *work* of fiction.[3]

The iterative quality of *Paradise*—"various events with various presenters"[4]—no doubt disorients some readers. To reorient readers toward ways of organizing and gaining control of the novel's "fictive heterocosm,"[5] Morrison prefigures the reader in *Paradise,* although she withholds that moment of orientation for nearly two-thirds of the novel. This prefiguration of the reader is a crucial aspect of Morrison's aesthetics— the shared responsibilities between author and reader. In this context, we are concerned with several readers: the participatory reader—Iser's implied reader and Morrison's cocreative reader—and the reader who participates outside the frame of narrative productivity where she/he engages in a recovery process. In this shared process, Morrison disrupts her own narrative in order to guide the reader toward a reconstruction of the text. Related to this participatory process is a recovery process that entails what Wayne Booth terms "critical re-reading," in which we "try to deepen or clarify the experience or to discover *how* the author managed to achieve the results we love, or why he or she did not achieve such results" (104– 5). Peter Rabinowitz rightly notes that "authors are quite explicit, even forceful, in the ways they direct us" (54). To steer her readers in the "right" direction, Morrison frequently inserts clear and sometimes subtle markers.[6] Following Morrison's lead when she states that she must "provide the places and spaces so that the reader can participate," and "because it is the affective and participatory relationship between the artist and the speaker and the audience that is of primary importance" ("Rootedness" 341), readers may find *Paradise* far less daunting on a second or guided reading.

A purposive reading of "Patricia," the sixth chapter in *Paradise*, offers the rewards of demystifying one of the most important moments in the novel and the intellectual work of unmasking the reader's involvement in and disengagement from Patricia's perspective in comprehending the novel's complexity. Patricia's "telling," "reading," "writing," and "interpreting" the history of Ruby orient the reader toward the novel and guide her/him toward her/his role in the narrative process. Even though Patricia is offered as a guide to the novel, the reader is expected to maintain "a privileged position" of "readerly expertise and readerly knowledge" (Dimock 119). Differently stated, the reader, though guided by Patricia's example, is expected to keep a certain distance from her and maintain an awareness that encompasses and transcends Patricia's. If the reader wishes to achieve the most efficacious interpretation of *Paradise*, she/he can neither ignore nor place total reliance on Patricia's project, an embedded narrative about writing and reading.

One function of this embedded story is to provide the reader with signals for making the connections between the nine named chapters and certain external events alluded to in the novel. Mieke Bal writes that "the embedded story can *explain* the primary story or it may *resemble* the primary story." For example, a character like Patricia can signal the relationship *explicitly* by "narrating the embedded story" or the reader may be left with the responsibility of locating the "hints" that indicate the relationship between the embedded text and the primary text (144). In *Paradise* the eponymous character of chapter 6 is a figuration of the reader, meant to aid in the telling, understanding, and interpretation of the novel as a whole.

As the figuration of the reader, Patricia occupies several positions. She holds a dual position within the community: she is an insider, a member of the elite 8-rocks on her father's side; and an outsider, the offspring of "tainted" blood on her mother's side. Through this dual status she is the reader's source for comprehensive information. Because of her unique perspective, she stands inside and outside and is therefore more perceptive: (1) she has unique access to information, (2) she is a guide to the history of the town, (3) she mirrors the reader's activity, and (4) she is the object of critical scrutiny. Because Patricia is so important to our interpretation of the novel, we are pushed to a gendered reading. In other words, Patricia's privileged position as guide to the community is a crucial link to the feminine perspectives.

When asked if *Paradise* is a "feminist" novel, Morrison responded, "Not at all. I would never write any 'ist' novels." Although Morrison resists the feminist label, she has nevertheless constructed a text in which gender predominates. And although she may "detest and loathe" "ists," does not "subscribe to patriarchy," and does not "think it should be substituted with matriarchy," Morrison does admit that the novel raises "a question of equitable access" (Jaffrey 5). After all, what is a reader to make of a text in which references to women often place them in positions where decisions are made for them by men and their actions often result from male oppression and violence? How does one interpret such moments where "women had no firm opinion" (17) until one of their own (another woman) died and they, with the consent of men, named their new town Ruby? Statements such as "The ladies promise to bring us coffee" (58), "I'm her father. I'll arrange her mind," and "[The men] bowed their heads and listened . . . to the tippy-tap steps of women who were nowhere in sight" (61) indeed call attention to gender-based roles. This accessibility to knowledge and female presence provided women in *Paradise* opens up possibilities for feminist readings. By activating silenced, marginalized, demonized, and brutalized female voices within a text constructed around male rule, Morrison, indeed, invites gender critique.[7]

Wai-Chee Dimock observes that "gender is most useful as an analytic category when it is understood to be constituted in time and constrained by time, propelled by temporal necessity and subject to temporal reconfiguration" (125). Dimock's notion of the temporality of gender is a useful precaution for analyzing *Paradise* from the perspective of the embedded reader. Dimock argues against any notion of a universal or essentialized gender: she views gender as a helpful strategy for reading when it is applied discretely and contextually. This application of gender can be located at the moment of disruption when *Paradise* invites generalized and particularized readings, moments in which men define and castigate women in order to control them: "Lord, I hate a nasty woman"; "I *know* they got powers" (275); "Bitches. More like witches"; "These here sluts out there by themselves never step foot in a church. . . . They don't need men and they don't need God" (276)—all inventions by men trying to build a case against a group of women and having a need to demonize women in order to control or destroy them. These are instances in which patriarchy invites not substitutional matriarchy but a scrupulous attention to gender and the differences it makes.

Patricia's name is rooted in the words "patrician" and "patriarchy," suggesting her hereditary link to the patrician families, the original founders of Haven/Ruby.[8] She is deeply conscious of her roots: on the one hand, desirous of exploiting that rootedness for communal recognition and, on the other hand, eager to expose the patriarchal oppression inherent in those roots. She is, on her father's side, a descendant of the original founders—Cato and Blackhorse. On the maternal side she has mixed blood. Her mother, Delia, a woman "with no last name," "without [a] people," a woman with "sunlight skin," a woman with "racial tampering" (197) and an outsider from Tennessee, "looked like a cracker and was bound to have cracker-looking children like [Patricia]" (196).

In another sense, Patricia is a "patriarchal" figure in the community by virtue of her role as the town's principal teacher—preceded by the Morgan sisters, Dovey and Soane—now assisted by Anna Flood and Richard Misner. Patricia is also the town's unofficial historian. Her accounts of events are corroborated and/or referenced by other characters. The narrator observes that when Lone tries to fathom events she looks for signs in nature, the "obvious," "something more profound than Morgan memory or Pat Best's history book" (272). Steward Morgan's unarticulated thoughts about Patricia's history project surface when the subject of the disappearance of Patricia's daughter is discussed: "No major loss if she did run off. Serves Pat right, he thought. She noses about in everybody's business but clams up if you get near hers" (123). Steward's characterization of Patricia is borne out in her conversation with Richard and in her unexpressed thoughts at Save-Marie's funeral.

Patricia's narrative reveals a critical and speculative mind that emulates the reader's orientation toward the text. In her attempts to resurrect and recognize the roles of women in Haven and Ruby, Patricia mirrors Morrison's project of giving voice to nine women (a counter and contemporary narrative to the narrative about the nine original families of Haven/Ruby designated by male surnames and male leaders). By giving voice to these women, Morrison does not seek to silence or displace male voices; rather, she provides appositional narratives to complement and revise the male narratives that have either ignored or presumed to speak for women. This decision is not unlike Morrison's decision in *Beloved* to place Paul D's narrative next to Sethe's (273).[9]

Consider the various accounts of the storming of the Convent. Patricia offers three versions of what happened there in July 1976: "two editions of the official story" (296) and a third version, to which only the reader is privy—"her own." One male account accuses and attempts to exonerate "nine men [who] had gone to talk to and persuade the Convent women to leave or mend their ways; there had been a fight, the women took other shapes and disappeared into thin air." The second official (male) version accuses five men and depicts four others as defenders of the women who "attacked" them (296–97). Patricia's own version mimics the reader's critical gesture of trying to reconcile the various accounts of what happened: "that nine 8-rocks murdered five harmless women (*a*) because the women were impure (not 8-rock); (*b*) because the women were unholy (fornicators at the least, abortionists at most); and (*c*) because they *could*—which was what being 8-rock meant to them and was also what the 'deal' required" (297). What is true for the reader, who has by now heard all accounts of the raid, is that all motives are plausible within the context of the male-dominated town of Ruby, but Patricia's interpretation seems closest to the truth of what actually occurred and why. Patricia's penchant for gathering and interpreting information keeps her alert to whatever goes on in and around town. While she is not "privy to many people's confidences, Pat gathers from talks with her father, with Kate [Golightly] and from deliberate eavesdropping that four months" after the Convent raid the leaders of Ruby "were still chewing the problem, asking God for guidance if they were wrong" (298). In other words, the narratives the men had devised to cover their crime had not held up under the community's scrutiny.

The text astutely corroborates and challenges Patricia's interpretation by allowing Richard and Anna to observe the aftermath of the raid. Anna's conclusion about what had occurred at the Convent is as crucial to the reader's interpretation as Patricia's is, since Patricia's interpretation is based on hearsay and speculation. Anna's presence at the scene after the crime allows another woman's voice to challenge the men's versions. Anna also sees the "terribleness" the men saw, but what the men interpret as "pornography" and "Satan's scrawl," Anna reads "instead [as] the turbulence of females trying to bridle, without being trampled, the monsters that slavered them" (303). The importance of Anna's visit to the scene cannot be overstated in the context of Patricia's role as embedded reader. This eyewitness account reminds us that the truth is subject to scrutiny, a fact emphasized when Anna "examin[ed]" the scene of slaughter "as closely as her lamp permitted" (303). Again the nudge to the reader: we can discern only as far as our eyes can see—but not always clearly and accurately. As readers we need to be alert to various accounts of events in *Paradise* and, coextensively, to everything we read and see and hear—and most especially to what we think we know.

But what we do know from Anna's assessment of the scene is that Anna's insight is much closer to the reality of what had gone on at the Convent prior to the raid. Thus, beyond her alliance with Patricia, the distant observer, Anna is able to read the drawings on the cement floor as expressions of the interior lives of the women who occupied the Convent. Her remarks, therefore, lead the reader back to Consolata's narrative and the scene of exorcism. But this scene can only be understood after we have completed most of the novel, since it appears in the chapter immediately following Patricia's chapter. Numerous signs point to four drifters—Mavis, Seneca, Pallas, and Gigi—and their relationship to Consolata, who has grown weary of their dependence on her as "ideal parent, friend, companion in whose company they were safe from harm" (262), and who has a desire to expose her own demons. The women, in self-expressive poses, lie on the cellar floor while Consolata traces their naked images and then directs them to hold their poses without speaking. It is this ritual exposure of their bodies as mere flesh, shadowing their interior lives, that prompts the women to speak their pain and, through the drawings on their silhouettes, to explore and expose their inner selves—an exploration and an exposure that begin with Consolata's narrative of her past, a narrative that releases the other women to share their stories. This private space, known only to the five women, has been their site of confession, contrition, and expiation: "Life, real and intense, shifted to down there" (264). These shadow images of themselves have become such virtual realities to their revitalized selves that they must "be reminded of [their] moving bodies" (265). And "with Consolata in charge . . . feeding them bloodless food and water alone to quench their thirst, they altered" (265). The interior changes seem to occur in inverse relation to the women's ability to speak their "sins" and "crimes."

The reader's circuitous journey through this scene of female exorcism and recovery from physical and psychological abuses reveals how we can and often do misread. The conflicting interpretations of the images can at least be measured against those of the women responsible for those images inasmuch as they are witnesses to the actual inscriptions; yet even they must ask one another what the images mean; they do not make assumptions about each other's inscriptions. Their resistance to assumptions evinces a far deeper appreciation for self-expression and self-definition than that which many outside the Convent accord the women. For example, when Pallas draws a picture of a baby in the stomach of her shadow image, the others ask if the father is Carlos or one of the boys who gang-raped her. Pallas responds by drawing "next to the baby a picture of a woman's face with . . . a crooked fluffy mouth" to which she adds "two long fangs" (265). This act is followed by silence. The reader, like the women, is left to fathom Pallas's intentions and meaning. That the ritual works is evidenced by Seneca's cessation of self-mutilation, which had begun when she was a child in a foster home—where she had been molested by another child, leading to her conviction that "there was something inside her that made boys snatch her and men flash her" (261)—and her decision "to mark the open body lying on the cellar floor" (265). Hence, the act of self-mutilation transmuted to a shadow drawing has been misread or correctly interpreted by different spectators. Similar transmutations of self-loathing and self-blame happen for Mavis, who faces her responsibility in the inadvertent suffocation of her twins; for Pallas, who can now confront the repressed memories of losing her lover Carlos to her mother and the ordeal of gang rape; for Gigi, who confronts the incest with her father; and finally for Consolata, the initiator of the ritual confessions by sharing her own losses. In time the Convent women are "no longer haunted" but are "calmly themselves" (266).

Through these interpretive acts, the text steers the reader toward a deeper understanding and more valid interpretation of the Convent women. Although Patricia and Anna have pieces of the truth and the men have invented narratives to support their crime, only the reader can bear witness to the truth by filling in the gaps left by Patricia's insinuations and Anna's intuition.

Patricia's chapter also provides an appropriate starting place for analyzing Morrison's narrative intentions in *Paradise*. The intratextual references coalesce and disperse in this chapter much like the coalescence of the "blood rule" to which Patricia's body and personal history attest. Her chapter is not, however, the novel in miniature or a summary of the novel's events. Patricia's narrative is a signal for reconceptualizing and reordering events in the textual world, a process of "simultaneous decomposing and enabling" (Iser, *Fictive Imaginary* 234). Focusing on the subject of Patricia's "project" and on Patricia as one "subject," a focalized character in *Paradise,* the reader discovers links that illuminate the other woman-identified chapters. One way to unravel some of the density of the text is to view Patricia's narrative as a device for orienting the reader toward textual signification and to view Patricia as a character for the reader to scrutinize in the context of the larger story.

Cast as Ruby's teacher-historian, Patricia serves as the reader's guide to and through Haven and Ruby. She is also a temporary consciousness through which the reader comes to know and better understand the interconnectedness of the host of characters in *Paradise*. Each of Patricia's narrative positions functions in direct relation to the reader's role as participant in narrative construction. When Patricia's discourse is appropriated by the narrator, we are aware that we are getting two versions of Patricia—hers and someone else's. The text alerts us to the conflation of Patricia's and the narrator's voices in the following representative passage:

"Because [Patricia's father] had wanted to be, studied to be, a doctor, most of his enterprises had to do with operating on the sick or dead. . . . [Patricia] wished he had been a doctor, had been accepted at medical school. Chances are her mother would be alive today." But "Maybe not. Maybe he would have been away at Meharry instead of the mortuary school when Delia died" (186–87).[10] This example is typical of Morrison's elision of the narrator's perspective and a character's language and thoughts—a process she employs throughout the text. This strategy minimizes interruptions in the narrative flow by limiting direct speech while simulating the character's language through the narrative voice.

The conflation of voice and the language of the quoted passage are also cues for the reader: What are the connections between the mortuary school and Meharry Medical School? Had Roger Best been in Nashville he would have been too far away to prepare his wife's and stillborn daughter's bodies for burial. The information that clues us to this critical difference is the community's disgust with Roger Best's actions in this regard. But "father or no father, husband or no husband, you both had to go in the ground," Patricia writes (198)[11]—her simulation of direct speech. Patricia's analysis of the town's attitude toward her parents is corroborated by others. When Richard asks Anna "why folks freeze around [Roger Best]," and when he wonders whether their behavior is due to his "mortuary business," Anna suggests, "Probably. That and, well, he 'prepared,' if you get my meaning, his own wife" (118). Roger's granddaughter, Billie Delia, is also aware that the town "had tried to ruin [him], succeeded in swallowing her mother and almost broken her own self" (308) had she not left town, seeking shelter first at the Convent and then settling in Demby, a nearby town. These comments outside Patricia's purview lend credibility to her conclusions about her family's partial isolation within the community.

Patricia's dual status of insider/outsider is revealed in a conversation with Richard, a local minister and newcomer to Ruby, who, along with Anna, teaches "Negro History every Thursday afternoon" (209). Richard is a civil rights activist who had been arrested and "jailed with thirty-eight others in a tiny cell in Alabama" (205) and now is concerned about Ruby's isolationism, especially in its refusal to get involved in the civil rights movement when African American students are arrested for civil protests in nearby Norman, Oklahoma. He is behind the youths' rebellion and challenge to authority in Ruby. He is also concerned that Patricia may not be giving her students "enough" history: "Did she think education was knowing enough to get a job?" He notes that even though she "didn't seem to trust these Ruby hardheads with the future any more than he did, but neither did she encourage change." So when Richard suggests that Patricia "despises Africa," her reply gives the reader a great deal of information about herself and the extent to which she may have been corrupted by a system that purports to privilege African blood: "[Africa] just doesn't mean anything to me" (209). Patricia's words recall Soane's notion of Africa, which "was the seventy-five cents she gave to the missionary society collection. She had the same level of interest in Africans as they had in her: none" (104). When Richard further presses Patricia, "What does mean something to you?" she answers, "The periodic chart of the elements and valences" (209). What the reader discovers about Patricia in this exchange is revealing: she has a myopic view of history (witness her history of Ruby), and she wants something stable, immutable, reliable—some certainties: things her insider/outsider status cannot offer her. In place of a stable and an immutable history, her relationship to her community has produced in her a deep cynicism. Patricia is an example of the individual with narrow politics—she critiques patriarchy and class but has a blind spot when it comes to interracial racism. She has split affinities toward her family and the leaders of the community but has no interest in or empathy for the youth struggling to combat the racism within the Commonwealth of Oklahoma.

When she finds herself in tears at Save-Marie's funeral, Patricia dons her historian's mask and becomes "her familiar, dispassionately amused self." Then we are reminded that Patricia's view of herself may not necessarily comport with the view others have of her and that she may have doubts about who she really is. After all, "the absence of a eulogy" for the young child "had made her cry" (296). The attempt to recover her mask of dispassionateness reminds us that Patricia is not all she appears to be. Moreover, Patricia herself is uncertain about her attitude and feelings: "At least she *hoped* she was dispassionate, and *hoped* amusement was what she was feeling" (emphasis added). Although Patricia views herself as "a scholar, not a romantic," she is aware of "other views about her attitude, some of which Richard . . . had expressed ('Sad. Sad and cold')" (296). The insertion of Patricia's moment of self-reflection reminds us that Patricia is not totally reliable as a historian, that she, like a reader, can be subjective and biased, and that interpretation is not an objective act grounded in the text alone; it also lies somewhere between the text and the reader's perception of the text.

Configured as the intellectual—probing facts and esoteric histories—Patricia refracts the reading process and draws the reader into her project. As the text's mediating figure, she invites trust even though we recognize that much of her history is speculative. Words and phrases such as "gleaned," "she gave up all pretense to objective comment," "where proof was not available she interpreted—freely," "I bet," and "or so Pat supposed" (187–93) remind us that Patricia's interpretations, like our own, are subject to further scrutiny, revision, and other interpretations. But her theories are sometimes plausible and comforting to readers in search of a "map" to Ruby. When Patricia studies and updates her history of Ruby, we are involved with her on multiple levels—as genealogist, chronicler, reader, critic, and interpreter. Positioned as a passive observer, Bal notes that "the reader watches with the character's eyes and will, in principle, be inclined to accept the vision presented by that character" (104). The reader is blocked from complete reliance on Patricia's perspective when the narrator suggests that Patricia believes that "she alone had the required emotional distance. She alone would figure out why a line was drawn through Ethan Blackhorse's name in the Blackhorse family Bible and what the heavy ink blot hid next to Zechariah's name in the Morgan Bible" (188). What is most evident is that Patricia's history of Ruby must be read with cautious skepticism.

The reader may, at first, be inclined to accept the accuracy of Patricia's ordered and labored "research"—factual, factoidal, inventive, and speculative—because it may provide some relief from the densely verbal morass of the earlier chapters and because it offers a salutary, less frustrating approach to reading the text as a whole. Reading Patricia's narrative, the reader discovers an opportunity to gather and organize her/his own thoughts in some relational and reconstructive fashion about the discrete and intersecting narratives preceding it and the three following. Reading Patricia's "history" of Ruby, the reader can reconsider, reorder, and reevaluate her/his understanding of the other parts of *Paradise*. Patricia's narrative, on the one hand, restores the reader's balance and perspective on the text; on the other hand, it gives the reader a sense of mastery of the text—a degree of readerly competence—and ultimately a limited understanding of the various histories in the novel.[12] Her narrative is the point at which the earlier parts of the novel become material for each reader's history.

If Patricia stands in for and alongside the reader and the reader stands outside Patricia's field of vision, how do these parallel and complementary readings complicate our reading of Patricia as one of the Ruby women? If there is a relationship between the author/narrator and the embedded and the implied reader, how does that relationship enable the politics of gender? The answers to these questions inhere in our reading of Patricia's narrative as discrete and parallel to the other narratives. Patricia herself is part of the answer to the question she raises in her history project:

"Who were these women, who like her mother, had only one name? Celeste, Olive, Sorrow, Ivlin, Pansy? Who were these women with generalized last names? Brown, Smith, Rivers, Stone, Jones. Women whose identity rested on the men they married—if marriage applied: a Morgan, a Flood, a Blackhorse, a Poole, a Fleetwood" (187–88). Although Patricia's question is directed toward the deceased wives and relatives of the original settlers of Haven, the reader might phrase the question in the present tense to ask about the names that signal the nine chapters of *Paradise.* Who are these women with suggestive first names—"Ruby," "Mavis," "Grace," "Seneca," "Divine," "Patricia," "Consolata," "Lone," and "Save-Marie"—and with tenuous links to and disconnections from families and communities?

Who *is* Patricia? How does the reader define her in relation to self and community? Does she have agency and power? Is her history project an expression of her desire for agency? Answers to these questions are discovered when the reader ceases to be a passive participant—as "Patricia's follower" as she reads and writes and interprets her community—and becomes an active participant—as a reader who has learned from Patricia how to make stories and how to narrate them. This shift in the reader's focalization is an appositional and complementary reading of Patricia as a character, which is to say that Patricia is no longer directing the reader's focus; she is now the object of the reader's theories. This switch occurs when Patricia completes her latest notations on her family tree. This shift is accomplished by placing Patricia in a space where the reader can observe her actively engaged in self-revealing conversations.

The details in Patricia's written words to her deceased mother reveal more about herself, about the history of Ruby, and about the devious and deadly consequences of the blood rule: "You must have believed that deep down they hated you, but not all of them, maybe not none of [the Ruby women], because they begged the men to go to the Convent for help. Even with their wives begging they came up with excuses." Patricia speculates that the "8-rock men didn't want to go and bring a white into town; or else didn't want to drive out to a white's house begging for help; or they just despised [Delia's] pale skin so much they thought of reasons why they could not go" (198). We learn from Patricia and through the corroboration of others that Roger and Delia are not the only ones ostracized because of the blood rule: "Look what they did to Menus, forcing him to give back or return the woman he brought home to marry. The pretty sandy-haired girl from Virginia" (195). Lone offers a similar version when she tries to fathom Menus's participation in the Convent raid: "Maybe it was just to erase the shame he felt at letting Harper and the others talk him out of marrying that woman he brought home. That pretty redbone girl they told him was not good enough for him; said she was more like a fast woman than a bride" (277–78). The blood rule is most absurdly articulated when Deek Morgan worries that the body parts shipped from battle may not all belong to his sons; he instructs Roger to "get rid of the white pieces" if "all the parts" are not "black" (112). Lone's and Deek's comments, occurring outside Patricia's chapter, give further credibility to Patricia's skin theory. Such comments are evidence of subtle opposition to the blood rule and proof Patricia has silent allies who, like her, do not share this opposition with other members of the town.

When Patricia speaks to her father, writes to her mother, or speaks with Richard, these characters pull from her aspects of her personality and feelings that we might not otherwise be privy to. Her queries about the town's excluding her family from participation in the annual Christmas pageant, which replicates the journey of the nine families from Mississippi and Louisiana to Oklahoma, evince Patricia's desire for a closer communal connection. "It was skin color, wasn't it? . . . The way people get chosen and ranked in this town?" (216), Patricia asks her father, simultaneously exposing her desire to be intimately connected to the community and her realization that she is set apart from it. The revelation that her family is excluded because she is not an 8-rock—a black distinguished by putatively untainted African blood—disturbs Patricia. As readers we, like Patricia, have to question the authenticity of the blood rule when we learn that the Blackhorses have long straight hair. Patricia also notes that blood rules lead to all kinds of complications, including incest, or what she terms an "invisible glitch" (196). The following passage reveals both these complications and Patricia's history:

> I know all of the couples wanted preacher-attended marriages, and many had them. But there were many others that practiced what Fairy DuPres called "takeovers." A young widow might take over a single man's house. A widower might ask a friend or a distant relative if he could take over a young girl who had no prospects. Like Billy's family. His mother, Fawn, born a Blackhorse, was taken over by his grandmother's uncle, August Cato. Or, to put it another way, Billy's mother was wife to her own great-uncle. Or another way: my husband's father, August Cato, is also his grandmother's (Bitty Cato Blackhorse's) uncle and therefore Billy's great-granduncle as well. (Bitty Cato's father, Sterl Cato, took over a woman named Honesty Jones. It must have been she who insisted on naming her daughter Friendship, and she was probably riled at hearing the child called Bitty the rest of her life). (196)

This passage combines facts and conjecture. It reveals Patricia's attempt to interpret the past in light of present knowledge and events. Moreover, the passage exposes Patricia's cynicism and implicit bitterness toward the leaders of Ruby and their ruling doctrine. The cynicism and bitterness are evident in her analysis of the invisible effects of the blood rule: "Since Bitty Cato married Peter Blackhorse, and since her daughter, Fawn Blackhorse, was wife to Bitty's uncle, and since Peter Blackhorse is Billy Cato's grandfather—well, you can see the problem with blood rules" (196). Patricia speculates that compulsory intracommunal marriages can lead to implosion—to depopulation by low birthrates and insanity due to inbreeding and abandonment of community by young women like Billie Delia. Patricia theorizes that her husband, Billy Cato, was an only child because "August Cato shunned temptation or any thought of looking outside the families. . . . Maybe his advanced age was why [his wife Fawn] had just one child" (197). Patricia's "any thought" hints at the social and political pressures that maintain tight control over community members and their posterity.

The chapter ends with Patricia's recognition that "everything that worries" the town leaders "must come from women" (217), or, as Anna, a descendant of the original founders who spent most of her life in Detroit, slyly notes, the message carved on the lip of the Oven means "Be the Furrow of *Her* [not His] Brow" (159). Patricia's and Anna's observations corroborate and invite a closer scrutiny of the men's reasons for storming the Convent. We learn in the first chapter, "Ruby," what the men think of the residents of the Convent as they enter the kitchen: "Slack . . . August just around the corner and these women [at the Convent] have not even sorted, let alone washed, the jars" (5). On the other hand, the Ruby leaders believe "there wasn't a slack or sloven woman anywhere in [Ruby]" because "from the beginning its people were free and protected" (8). Protected by whom? And at what cost to their freedom and selfhood? Since the Convent women are free and beyond the "protection" of the Ruby men, they must be inferior in character to the women of Ruby and must, therefore, be demonized so that they can be "legitimately" destroyed.[13] Lone later observes that "neither [Deacon nor Steward Morgan] put up with what he couldn't control" (278–79)—the Morgans being the primary leaders by virtue of their wealth and the primacy of their family, at least in terms of the oral and mythical history they have created around the ancestral Zechariah Morgan. Ruby, with its "quiet white and yellow houses full of industry; and in them were elegant black women at useful tasks; orderly cupboards minus surfeit or miserliness; linen laundered and ironed to perfection; good meat seasoned and ready for roasting" (111), is idealized by Deek. Steward, honing his anger and providing himself a motive for attacking the Convent women, counterposes a demonic image of the Convent women against a romantic vision of the "ladies" of the original community called Haven: "The women of the Convent were for him a flaunting parody of the nineteen Negro ladies of his and his brother's youthful memory and perfect understanding. They were the degradation of that moment they'd shared of sunlit skin and verbena. . . . He could not abide them for sullying his personal history with their streetwalkers' clothes and whores' appetites" (279). The phrase "perfect understanding" reminds the reader of the men's commitment to an ideal they have constructed out of a highly romanticized and bitter past.

Purporting to appreciate women's industry, these men nevertheless ignore the evidence of productive women-identified activities before them. The Convent women "have been taken by surprise," taken in the midst of their labor. Witness the "full pitcher of milk," "four bowls of shredded wheat," "scallion piled high like a handful of green confetti," "bone white potatoes, wet and crisp," and "stock [that] simmers on the stove," while "a dozen loaves of bread swell" (5). In this economy of patriarchal values, the Ruby men's devaluation, or deliberate oversight, of the Convent women's work—the utility of it—reveals their hypocrisy and avowed purpose. For these men, the Convent women are contaminating evil; hence, everything connected with them must be corrupt. These women are, as the Ruby men would have us believe, by their very nature corrupt, and by virtue of their corruption they are corrupting. Within the context of evil personified, the Convent women, if one accepts the rationalizations of the Ruby leaders, pose a threat to the moral stability of Ruby. Patricia's observation that the men fear the Convent women is borne out in the men's decision to destroy them. Thus, the Ruby men, under the guise of protecting the purity of their community's blood, must idealize their own women and demonize the Convent women.

Like Patricia, who views herself as a dispassionate scholar, the Morgans, the main movers and shakers of Ruby, believe they alone know the true history and purpose of Haven and Ruby societies. Yet their construction of narratives around women without agency (Ruby women) or women beyond the scope of their "legitimate" power (the Convent women) attests to the patriarchal privilege they have accrued over the years. Steward's wife, Dovey, has internalized the men's attitude toward the Convent women and has become estranged from her twin, Soane, as a result. "People talk about them all the time, though. Like they were slime," according to Dovey. To Soane's admonition that "these are women . . . just women," Dovey counters, "Whores, though, and strange, too" (288). In her anguish and confusion, engendered, no doubt, by the loss of numerous infants, Sweetie also reacts to what she has probably heard from her husband, Jeff. In the middle of the night, driven by neurotic pressures from stillbirths and infant deaths, Sweetie heads for the Convent. Encountering Seneca, who is also headed for the Convent, Sweetie thinks, "Sin. . . . I am walking next to sin and wrapped in its cloak [Seneca's serape]." To Sweetie, the women "seemed like birds, hawks." Later, when she wakes in the Convent and one of the "hawks" speaks to her "the way a demon would," Sweetie "call[s] on her Savior"—the name, according to Christian myth, that overpowers the devil (129). Sweetie's internalization of the demonic is a manifestation of the men's power to control and corrupt the thinking of some of the women in the town.

But Sweetie's and Dovey's voices are countered by Billie Delia's when she brings Pallas Truelove to the Convent after Pallas has been gang-raped: "Don't be afraid. . . . Of them [the Convent women], I mean. . . . A little nuts, maybe, but loose, relaxed, kind of. . . . They'll take care of you or leave you alone—whichever you want" (175–76). Billie Delia's description of the Convent women reminds us that Billie Delia herself had spent time at the Convent and that "they were nice to [her]. Nicer than—well, very nice" (176). Enough said, she implies, and enough to give the lie to the men's claims about the Convent women. In these exchanges the reader recalls and reassesses the scattered pieces of the narrative connecting the Convent and Ruby in order to maintain a balanced view—though not a necessarily unbiased interpretation—of events and points of view.

Dovey's and Sweetie's sentiments reveal their internalization of their husbands' attitude toward the Convent women while reminding us of a historical parallel—the New England Puritans and the Salem witch trials. Like the New England Puritans, who were "transported by the vision of a more godly society than the one they had known" and who "quickly encountered the difficulties of trying to escape the past" (Tally 63–68),[14] the founders and leaders of Haven and Ruby see their mission as a divine calling to establish an inviolate and inviolable black community. The Ruby leaders, like the New England Puritans, discover that there are some among them who do not "share the founders' beliefs and goals" (Karlsen 185–86). The leaders' desire and efforts to keep the town inviolable from outside and from within are evident in Patricia's project and in the intergenerational actions of Morgans. Carol Karlsen has noted that among the New England Puritans men were more likely to articulate "beliefs" and were the primary accusers concerning witchcraft (222), while those accused were "primarily women who had violated gender norms" and "were thought to have committed fornication, infanticide, or other sexually related offenses" or who had inherited property (196). The Ruby men's motives are suggested in Patricia's narrative—"The generations had to be not only racially untampered with but free of adultery too" (217)— and reinforced in Lone's.

These violations of communal norms undermine the leaders' credibility and expose their need to hide their hypocrisy by attempting to cover their adulterous behavior. Such violations reveal the men's willful denial of the Ruby women's ostensibly "evil" conduct—especially Arnette's and Soane's. The fear of exposure and their inability to control the youth of the town and some of their women—Soane and Arnette, for example— compel the men to cry "witchcraft." J. Brooks Bouson observes that "as the Convent becomes the repository of the scandalous secrets of the respectable 8-rocks, the people of Ruby come to perceive the Convent women as potentially dangerous" (203). Lone, the one surviving female from the original settlers of Haven, overhears the "evidence" the leaders mount against the Convent women: "I caught them kissing on each other in the back of that ratty Cadillac. . . . two more was fighting over them in the dirt"; "My wife says they did an abortion on her"; "Roger . . . said the girl he dropped off there [at the Convent] was openly flirting with him"; "[Arnette] thinks they kept her baby and told her it was stillborn"; "I *know* they got powers" (275). The "evidence" accrues: Billie Delia is said to have "knocked her mama down the stairs and took off for that place [the Convent] like a shoat hunting a teat" (276). These actions, according to the court of male opinion, condemn the women as witches. When one man calls them bitches, he amends his epithet, "More like witches" (276). The reader recalls that Arnette had gone to the Convent seeking an abortion, which she herself had failed to induce with a "mop handle inserted with a rapist's skill" (250), in order to enter college on schedule; that Soane had sought assistance in inducing a miscarriage or abortion: "I can't have this child" (239), Soane importunes Consolata, the woman she realizes is having an affair with her husband; that "Seneca had arranged Pallas in her arms, rubbing the goose-bumpy arms" (165) because Pallas was ill; and that Gigi had provoked the fight with Mavis: "Gigi knew Mavis' touchy parts: anything insulting to Connie and any reference to her fugitive state" (168). This random sighting of four of the Convent women by a driver from Ruby becomes "evidence" for convicting and lynching them. Lone adduces from "handcuffs" and a rope that "the men had not come there merely to rehearse. Like boot camp recruits, like invaders preparing for slaughter, they were there to rave, to heat the blood or turn it icicle cold the better to execute the mission" (280).

The reader is asked to question this mission: "They think they have outfoxed the whiteman when in fact they imitate him. They think they are protecting their wives and children, when in fact they are maiming them. And when the maimed children ask for help, they look elsewhere for the cause" (306). These men are repeating one of the heinous crimes of the past: they are modeling for their women and children the actions of lynchers against innocent and powerless targets, in this case a few women. There are nine men against four women—"over twice the number of the women they are obliged to stampede or kill and they have the paraphernalia for either requirement: rope, a palm leaf cross, handcuffs, Mace and sunglasses, along with clean handsome guns" (3). The "palm leaf cross," resonant of the Ku Klux Klan's cross, and other paraphernalia render the scene all too familiar—a black version of a white lynching. But instead of a lone black male suspended from a tree above a fire, we have the body of an innocent white woman lying upon a "sacrificial" table. The text is unambiguous: black men have learned and repeated white men's most heinous crimes and, as one of them says, "Now we got white law on us as well as damnation" (290). This scene depicts men whose actions against women represent, on the surface, at least, "official" and "divine" sanction (the palm leaf cross), control (handcuffs, a rope, mace), and violence (guns). The excessive piety with which the Ruby men build their case against the Convent women is undercut by the extreme measures they use to attack them.

Karlsen also notes that in Puritan New England "most of the accused were women who had no brothers or sons, women who either had inherited or were likely to inherit property" (196). Once the women were accused and condemned, their property was auctioned, and who but men had the power and means to bid on that property? Lone's musings on the motivation of several participants in the "witch hunt" underscore the text's evocation of Puritan New England: "Sargent, she knew, would be nodding at every shred of gossip, chewing on the rag end of truth and wondering aloud why this deliberately beautiful town governed by responsible men couldn't remain so: stable, prosperous, with no back-talk young people. . . . But he would be thinking how much less his outlay would be if he owned the Convent land, and how, if the women are gone from there, he would be in a better position to own it." In fact, Sargent "had already visited the Convent" and had "offered to buy the place"; when the women refused to sell, he had advised them to "think carefully" because "other things could happen to lower the price" of their land (277). Sargent's response to the women's refusal to sell the Convent suggests that had this veiled threat been uttered by one of the Convent women it might have been part of the accumulated "evidence" against them. Karlsen points out that in colonial New England a "witch's grumbling words or thinly veiled threats following an argument were taken as evidence" (7). In borrowing the tools of white patriarchy, the black patriarchs of Ruby unwittingly perpetuate racism and in doing so are twice victimized: by the system they uncritically emulate and by their own racist and gendered politics. This adherence to a white patriarchal system simultaneously oppresses women and denies black men their full humanity. This evocation of the Salem witch hunt is best expressed in Audre Lorde's critique of patriarchy and women's desire for gender equality: "What does it mean when the tools of a racist patriarchy are used to examine the fruits of the same patriarchy? It means that the most narrow perimeters of change are possible and allowable" (110–11). If we place the Ruby men's conduct in the context of Lorde's critique, it is clear that much has not changed in terms of leadership. Richard, the outsider within and Morrison's choice as the moral consciousness within the male enclave, keenly aware of Ruby's failed vision, meditates on the town's origin and present condition: "Born out of an old hatred, one that began when one kind of black man scorned another kind and that kind took the hatred to another level, their selfishness had trashed two hundred years of suffering and triumph in a moment in such pomposity and error and callousness it froze the mind. Unbridled by Scripture, deafened by the roar of its own history, Ruby . . . was an unnecessary failure. . . . Soon Ruby will be like any other country town: the young thinking of elsewhere; the old full of regret." Richard wonders if "this hard-won heaven defined only by absence of the unsaved, the unworthy and the strange" can survive intact. If the failure lies with the leaders, "Who will protect [the people] from their leaders?" (306). If we accept Richard's assessment—and I think we should place it next to Patricia's and others', including our own—we come away with a not-so-promising future for Ruby: it will fall of its own dead weight of intolerance and insularity.

The assertion of the Convent as a female space and its implicit comparison to the Puritan New England forest recall a history of violations of women under the pretext of eradicating evil and ridding society of "detritus" and "venom" (4). This trope for unbridled violation of the Convent is a lust for power represented by the Morgans. The folly inherent in the Morgans' insistence on a community built on male dominance ballasted by a belief in racial purity—their unpolluted blackness—is difficult to sustain since the Morgans themselves are among the violators.

The destruction and/or "disappearance" of the Convent women is foreshadowed by Patricia's destruction of her history of Ruby: "Dear, dear God, I burned the papers" (217), the most detailed "history" of the women of Haven and Ruby. In doing so, Patricia, like the Ruby men, has effectively destroyed her self-incriminating "evidence" and ostensibly kept the community from knowing what she thinks and feels about them. But the reader may ask, now that we know the "official" and "unofficial" histories of the community, Is it necessary to preserve the names and lineages of all the people in Ruby since those histories, Patricia's included, are at best suspect? The "official history"—the "collection of family trees; the genealogies of each of the fifteen families"—was extracted from "Bibles" and "church records," which she had tried to fill in with unsuccessful attempts "to see letters and marriage certificates." The "official *story*," in contradistinction to the "official *history*"—an oral one—which is "elaborated from pulpits, in Sunday school classes and ceremonial speeches, had a sturdy public life" (188), while the "unofficial history" is gleaned from her "students' autobiographical compositions" (187), from names expunged from family Bibles. Still Richard wonders why the narratives of Ruby are narratives of the past: "Over and over and with the least provocation, they pulled from their stock of stories tales about old folks, their grands and great-grands; their fathers and mothers, dangerous confrontations, clever maneuvers. Testimonies to endurance, wit, skill, and strength. Tales of luck and outrage. But why were there no stories to tell of themselves? About their own lives they shut up. Had nothing to say, pass on. As though past heroism was enough of a future to live by. As though rather than children, they wanted duplicates" (161).

Richard's assessment of the Ruby leaders, including Patricia, is prompted by his dissatisfaction with their failure to live in the historical moment, to seize the moment when African Americans are negotiating and agitating for an end to racism. He is deeply concerned that Patricia's preoccupation with the past blinds her to the realities of the present and that the Ruby leaders would rather feed on past wrongs than seize the opportunity not just to be a part of history but to influence history. Readers must also question Richard's investment in contemporaneous history. As Michael Wood observes, it is not necessary "to distrust [Richard] to know we need to see the world from other angles" (118). Although Morrison admits that Richard is the character "closest to [her] own sensibility about moral problems" (Jaffrey 6), the reader must differentiate between Morrison the author and Morrison the potential reader looking at Richard as a character in a novel. Morrison the individual may be interested in the civil rights movement of the 1960s and 1970s, but Morrison the novelist has a much longer and more comprehensive view of history. It is even more important to remember that Richard, like Patricia, is temporally and historically motivated by self-interest.

Patricia's narrative is constructed along two historical axes: one, around two shameful periods in American history—colonial New England witchcraft and post-emancipation lynchings—draws parallels between history and the events that occur in the establishment of the towns of Haven and Ruby and the politics of nation building and social control. The other axis, the present, directs attention to the continuum of patriarchy in American society. In directing the reader's attention to Patricia's role as historian, two narrative moments have been captured here—the novelistic present and the historical past. In this economy of temporalities, we find two readers: the figural, Patricia, and the implied, the reader. *Paradise* paints a somewhat grim reality for black women and others confronting unrestrained black male power seeking to sustain itself under the law of the Founding Fathers, a rule embracing the founders and followers of colonial New England puritanism, the Klansmen, and the 8-rock dynasties of Haven and Ruby. In comparing the Convent women's situation to that of the women accused of witchcraft in colonial New England, the novel debunks the myth of the noble aims of the founding of what would eventually emerge as the United States of America. This picture is less grim if we accept the apotheosis or transubstantiation of the four women presumed murdered by the nine men storming the Convent: "Bodacious black Eves unredeemed by Mary, they are like panicked does leaping toward a sun that has finished burning off the mist and now pours its holy oil over the hides of game" (18). In staging the women's miraculous escape, Morrison posits a transcendent survivalist aesthetic that speaks to women's ability to overcome male oppression by whatever means necessary.

The use of women in and outside Ruby offers a contemporaneous counternarrative to the patriarchal narratives espoused by the leaders of Ruby. Thus, *Paradise,* generally, and Patricia's embedded text, particularly, demonstrate that the borders between history and fiction are not so clearly defined—that historical and fictional narratives are interpenetrative, enabling a deeper understanding of human relations. Beyond its interplay between fiction and history, *Paradise* reveals that reading is a process involving a close relationship between the author, the text, and the reader. Ultimately, the writing and interpretive processes are thrust upon us as readers who are asked to pause over our intellectual engagement with texts and examine what we do, how we do it, and why we do it.

5 *Reflections on the Ethics of Difference*

How lovely it is, this thing we have done—together.
—Toni Morrison, *Lecture and Speech of Acceptance,*
upon the Award of the Nobel Prize for Literature

In her Nobel Lecture, an allegory about language and the creative process, Morrison speaks about the ways in which language differentiates and sometimes divides humans: "Word-work is sublime [the old woman in the allegory] thinks because it is generative; it makes meaning that secures our difference, our human difference" (*Lecture and Speech* 22). This is, no doubt, the kind of word-work and wordsmith the Swedish Academy alluded to when it awarded Morrison the Nobel Prize and characterized her as "a literary artist of the first rank," as one who "delves into language itself, a language she wants to liberate from the fetters of race." In describing Morrison's artistic achievement, the academy spoke of her work as "finely wrought and cohesive, yet at the same time rich in variation. One can delight in her narrative technique, varying from book to book and developed independently" and suffused with "the luster of poetry" ("Nobel Prize," Oct. 1993). Poetic language reveals its luster in the context of some humanistic goal. This is the power and beauty of literary language that Martha Nussbaum has in mind when she writes that "there may be some views of the world and how one should live in it— views, especially, that emphasize the world's surprising variety, its complexity and mysteriousness, its flawed and imperfect beauty—that cannot be fully and adequately stated in the language of conventional philosophical prose, a style remarkably flat and lacking in wonder—but only in a language and in forms themselves more complex, more allusive, more attentive to particulars" (3).

The poetic luster of this unconventional language, a pattern that suffuses Morrison's oeuvre, helps shape her poetics of difference. In the Nobel Lecture, reflective of her ongoing concerns about difference, Morrison explores the fissures that often divide us. Compressed in this allegory are the conflicts that frustrate understanding and potentials for cooperative sharing. This allegory asks, What can people on opposite ends of a cultural divide learn from each other? The allegory takes a surprising twist. Instead of the proverbial ending in which young people are brought to their senses by the wisdom of an elder, in Morrison's version the goal is not to reinscribe the familiar but to surprise with the unanticipated. This allegory—as in the rest of Morrison's fiction a succession of narrative variations on a familiar and ever changing theme, one she has "heard . . . in the lore of several cultures"—enacts divisiveness by unfolding structures that explore the ethics of understanding through the aesthetics of difference.[1] Differentiating herself as a unique artist within a common artistic heritage, Morrison culturally identifies with the old woman, the "daughter of slaves, black, American, and [living] alone outside of town" (*Lecture and Speech* 9), the writer as Other existing on the margins with a voice insinuating itself into mainstream culture. She is likewise the elder within the ethnic community challenged by a younger generation:

> How dare you talk to us of duty when we stand waist deep in the toxin of your past? (27)

> Tell us what it means to be a woman so that we may know what it means to be a man. What moves at the margin. What it is to have no home in this place. To be set adrift from the one you knew. What it is to live at the edge of towns that cannot bear your company. (28–29)

The children's demand for a comprehensive historical narrative is prompted by the old woman's tossing the riddle of the bird (language) back into their interpretive sphere—"Whatever the case, it is your responsibility" (12)—and implying that answers to their queries lie not so much in the answers she may provide but in their own potential as writers. The answers also reside in the force of their questions—the desire to know, to understand, and to preserve the narratives that help to constitute who they are. The old woman, in lieu of a direct answer to their questions, offers a potential solution—"I trust you with the bird that is *not* in your hands because you have truly caught it"(30; emphasis added)—while reminding them that history/literature is a joint project: "How lovely it is, this thing we have done—together" (30).

A 1998 interview in London with Lana Wendt mirrors, in some respects, the Nobel Lecture, with its emphasis on location and subject matter. When Wendt asked Morrison if she ever intends to place white characters at the center of her fiction,[2] Morrison responded, "You can't understand how powerfully racist that question is, can you? . . . Because you could never ask a white author, 'When are going to write about black people?' Even the inquiry comes from a position of being in the center."[3] Morrison then paraphrased Wendt's question, "Is it possible that you'll ever enter the mainstream?" and added, "It's inconceivable that where I already am is the mainstream." After explaining her decision to write about blacks, Morrison went on to say with an edginess, "I stood on the border, stood on the edge, and claimed it as central and let the rest of the world come over to where I was." Wendt's question and recognition that Morrison was "profoundly unwavering on the black experience" changed what was, to that point, a routine interview into a dynamic exchange that reconfirmed Morrison's position regarding her decision to mine the African American experience as a valuable fictional source.

I want to call attention to the moral implications of that poetic quality, recognized by the Swedish Academy and identified by Wendt as the "dazzling style" of Morrison's "own creation": her ability to quicken—in a single utterance or textual moment—our moral sensibilities. To borrow from Noël Carroll, it is not so much that "narrative teaches us something brand new, but rather that it activates the knowledge and emotions, moral and otherwise, that we already possess" (141). A reflection on these statements should lead to a productive exploration of the ethical concerns of Morrison's work.

Before moving to these ethical concerns, I would like to point to another telling exchange in the Morrison-Wendt interview. Referring to her father's contempt for white people and his conviction that black people were "morally superior" to them, Morrison spoke about the "false security of the [racially] ostracized." Responding to Wendt's question of whether Morrison considered her own father a racist, Morrison answered affirmatively. The value of this exchange lies again in Wendt's desire for complicity in, perhaps, her own racism, but most assuredly in her need to feel that blacks can also be racists. Morrison's unblinking recognition of her father's racism is followed by her admission that she had found that her father had often been wrong about white people. Within Morrison's ethical landscape, it is evident that kinship does not mean closing one's eyes to reality. Morrison's convictions about the divisiveness of racism and other forms of prejudice have come as a consequence of living with a racist father and within a racist society. Attendant to these recognitions is her desire to expose and close the chasms created by all forms of prejudice.

By parsing Wendt's question about whites as mainstream characters in her fiction, Morrison forces Wendt to confront her unrecognized racism and to examine the world not from her secure mainstream position but from the margin—where she will see it from a different perspective. Although Wendt quickly defends the intent of her question, she exposes her own desire for inclusion in the fictional world of a writer of Morrison's stature. That the two women are speaking from different cultural positions is not the main concern of this project; what is of interest is the fact that these women are in agreement, even though their conversation suggests otherwise. Each speaks to Morrison's preoccupation with difference, though each approaches that difference from her separate and embodied sphere: Morrison from her fierce defense of the margin; Wendt in her concern to be recognized as a worthy subject by a writer of color.

What are we to make of this exchange of what seems, on one hand, to be an innocuous question and, on the other, a startling overreaction? Is one to accept, on the face of it, Wendt's explanation that she was referring to centrality of characters, not centrality of Morrison's artistic achievement? or Morrison's contention that Wendt's question is "powerfully racist"? The answer lies between their territorial positions. The exchange reveals a common desire expressed from two cultural perspectives: a white woman expressing a desire to see herself reflected in the work of a universally acclaimed writer and a black writer *hearing* that, until she incorporates white characters in her work, she is outside the mainstream. At least three fundamental issues emerge from this encounter: a breakdown in communication attributable to difference, a desire for representation, and an implied solution to their misunderstanding. These ostensibly competing positions are reflective of Morrison's life work—the conviction that African American lives have literary value and, therefore, deserve center stage, and any suggestion to the contrary must be confronted on those principles. Morrison's moral indignation prompted by Wendt's question is an excellent starting point for a discussion of the ethics of difference.

Susan Bordo, in speaking about the importance of trying to connect with other cultures, points to the importance of "recognizing, wherever one goes, that the other's perspective *is* fully realized, not a bit of exotic 'difference' to be incorporated within one's own world. The world-travelling thinker thus must be prepared not only to 'appreciate' the foreign, but also to recognize and nurture those places where worlds meet"; "the world-travelling thinker will always be ready to abandon familiar territory when human understanding and communication seem to require it" (287). The suggestion that one must enter the space of the other without attempting to change that space may seem simple enough, yet Morrison's passionate response to Wendt, unambiguous in its indictment of a perceived centrist position, reveals the urgency of Bordo's caveat. Bordo also points out the difficulty of trying to deconstruct dualism in culture:

> To be concretely—that is, culturally—accomplished requires that we bring the "margins" to the "center," that we legitimate and nurture, in those institutions from which they have been excluded, marginalized ways of knowing, speaking, being. Because relations of this sort are always concrete, historical events, enacted by real, historical people, they *cannot* challenge every insidious duality in one fell swoop, but neither can they reproduce exactly the same conditions as before "in reverse" . . . when we bring marginalized aspects of our identities (racial, gendered, ethnic, sexual) into the central arenas of culture they are themselves transformed and *transforming*. (42)

Admittedly, Wendt was not suggesting that Morrison abandon the margins; but she unwittingly implied, at least to Morrison, that her fiction contained a vacuum because it lacked mainstream characters.

A brief return to the Wendt interview reveals the classic convergence of race and desire. In her trenchant analysis of the implications of Wendt's question, Morrison returns to the site of her fiction and makes a powerful case for the centrality of the marginalized. From this pressure of exclusion, Morrison decided to mine African America for what it would yield about the human experience. This decision speaks to Morrison's faith in her ethnic community and in art as a vehicle for truth. The steadfastness of her vision—claiming the centrality of that marginal world—culminated in universal recognition, the Nobel Prize.

Fictional texts, according to Michael Kearns, through their power to "move the audience in some way," are "rhetorical" narratives. In what specific ways do "the elements of narrative actually work on readers?" (3) is a useful question for exploring the ways in which Morrison's fiction appeals to consciousness and conscience, a body of work that bears a decidedly moral suasion. Morrison's poetics of racism and prejudice invites a scrutiny of difference and the ways in which otherness affects relationships, while tweaking the reader's moral values by urging reflection and re-formation of attitudes and behavior. It is an appeal to those principles that speak to the humanity of all people. Of equal concern is the reader's attention to moral responsibility beyond diegesis and exegesis to self-examination.

Michael Taussig's observation of the interface of various races and classes in the Canal Zone during the construction the of the Panama Canal may shed some light on the way we look at Morrison's fictional construction of alterity. Taussig observes that, when dominant groups are forced to confront themselves as Other from the perspective of those they view as inferior, the refracted images of themselves may not be so flattering. Contemplating a Nigerian sculpture of a white man, Taussig writes, "For the white man, to read this face means facing himself as Others read him" and being "virtually forced to interrogate himself, to interrogate the Other in and partially constitutive of his many conflicting selves" (238). This refracted vision suggests another level of scrutiny when we interface with representations of self and Other in fictional texts. James I. Porter's musing on the disabled body prompts a similar reflection in the context of Morrison's exploration of difference: "Viewed in itself (an essentialized perspective—but that is part of the point), a disabled body seems somehow too *much* a body, too *real*, too corporeal: it is a body that . . . stands in its own way. From another angle, which is no less reductive, a disabled body appears to lack something essential, something that would make it identifiable and something to identify with; it seems too *little* a body: a body that is deficiently itself, not quite a body in the full sense of the word, not *real* enough" (13). In Morrison's fictional world, black bodies are often overdetermined and sometimes appear deficient; and from these ostensibly flawed bodies, Morrison's texts seek to create human beings longing to assume their "normal" place in the human family. Rosemarie Garland Thomson has noted that "America's aggregate history of racism and sexism . . . challenges the African American woman writer to produce a narrative of self that authenticates black women's oppressive history yet offers a model for transcending that history's limitations" (240). The disablements, birthmarks, discolorations, complexion—"material traces of racism" or "congenital variations upon which cultural otherness is built" (256)[4]—also signal a moral imperative for those who would devalue otherness.

"Every work of art," according to Leo Tolstoy, "results in the one who receives it entering into a certain kind of communion with one who produced or is producing the art, and with those who, simultaneously with him, before him, or after him, have received or will receive the same artistic impression" (38). Art should be "a belief in humanity and faith in its future," contends Marilyn French (76). The implications of these ways of reading are evident in Morrison's work, where she reminds us of the "power of embedded images and stylish language to seduce, reveal, and control" and their "capacity to help us pursue the human project—which is to remain human and to block the dehumanization of others" ("Strangers" 70). Following this lead, readers aware of injustices and reprehensible actions—regardless of the perpetrator's race, ethnicity, or gender—must surely condemn them. And even though a given text may not directly propose a program for dismantling racism and other forms of prejudice, Morrison's work, nevertheless, obliges the reader to search for clues to an implicit moral order. It is not enough, in Pecola's case, to empathize with a character's suffering; an ethical response would induce the reader's sense of fairness. It is insufficient to condemn injustice; it is equally important, whenever possible, to ameliorate it. Here, it is necessary to distinguish between guilt and conscience, between a sense of personal responsibility for some real or imagined wrong, and the sense that such wrongs can affect the well-being of those objectified and vilified because they are different—that "profoundly meaningful difference that requires a separation" that leaves the other "feeling soiled" (Wendt). In narrating injustice Morrison does not wish to stimulate white guilt or any other guilt in and of itself but to move beyond guilt toward constructive human encounters. Her work does more than call attention to the conditions that enable a profound sense of rejection; in highlighting certain details and privileging selected utterances, these texts rhetorically imply the responsibility to alter these conditions. To establish the grounds for these claims, I want to briefly recall several examples that open up the ethical imperatives of Morrison's work.

A Pecola Breedlove desiring to change the color of her eyes not only invites an indictment of the dominant culture but calls for recognition, especially by whites, of the suffering engendered by a racist alterity and the possibilities for altering the conditions that contribute to that suffering. This is what Noël Carroll calls a "*transactional* view," which stresses the "transaction between the narrative artwork and the moral understanding" (142). In this transaction, according to Carroll, we have an occasion "to deepen our grasp and our understanding of what we already know and in a way that also counts as learning . . . [and] grasping the significance of the connections between antecedently possessed knowledge" (143). It is not enough that readers recognize the harmful effects of one-dimensional images of beauty; it is also incumbent on them to discover how they are implicated in the perpetuation of such images. And, as Carroll notes, Morrison trusts the reader's "understanding of psychology" to determine the extent to which Pecola's condition "derives from her [mother's] displacement of her maternal concerns" to those of the white family. It is equally important that the reader experience the moral outrage "requisite to the text" (139).[5]

Similarly, when Guitar recalls the way his family was treated by the company boss after his father's accidental death on the job, we are asked to look at more than Guitar's harboring years of anger; we are urged to question the value the white boss places on a black life. When we read of Guitar's strong dislike for candy—a metaphor for the bitter sweetness of growing up black and the resistance to an oppression that seeks to sugarcoat the pain of blackness—we understand what he means when he says that sweets make him "think of dead people. And white people. And I start to puke." The description of the cause is morally persuasive in its transparency: "Since I was little [I have not liked sweets]. Since my father got sliced up in a sawmill and his boss came by and gave us kids some candy. Divinity. A big sack of divinity. His wife made it special for us. It's sweet, divinity is. Sweeter than syrup. Real sweet. Sweeter than . . ." (*Song* 61). Guitar punctuates his unfinished utterance by puking, a somatic expression of his moral repugnance toward the boss's insensitivity to his father's tragic death.[6] Milkman, however, is interested more in the effects of sugar on the body than in the boss's inappropriate response to the tragedy. The implications of the anecdote are intended primarily for the reader. Left as it is, with Guitar's inviting Milkman to join him for "some weed" (62), it remains for the reader to interpret the moral code embedded in Guitar's anecdote, since neither Guitar nor Milkman provides an explicit moral judgment. The anecdote offers ample material for discerning the root causes of Guitar's justifiable anger while questioning the appropriateness of his transferring his revulsion toward his father's boss to *all* white people.

In *Beloved,* when Sixo steals a shoat and then explains—"Sixo plant rye to give the high piece a better chance. Sixo take and feed the soil, give you more crop. Sixo take and feed Sixo give you more work"—we are told that "schoolteacher beat him anyway to show him that definitions belonged to the definers—not the defined" (190).[7] We, like the reluctant schoolteacher, may be struck by the cleverness of Sixo's reasoning, but the moral implications of his explanation emerge when we consider the conditions under which slaves were forced to work and sometimes impelled to subterfuge in order to survive as well as to maintain their humanity.

The slaveholder's morality is also at issue in Paul D's recapitulation of a scene in which his identity is thrown into relief as he tries to measure his freedom against a rooster's: "Mister, he looked so . . . free. Better than me. Stronger, tougher. Son of a bitch, couldn't even get out the shell by hisself but he was still king and I was . . ." Like Guitar, who is physically revulsed by the mere mention of divinity, Paul D "squeezed his left hand with his right . . . long enough for it and the world to quiet down and let him go." The notion that "Mister was allowed to be and stay what he was" and that he "wasn't allowed to be and stay what [he] was" is, for Paul D, unfathomable and unconscionable. "Schoolteacher changed me. I was something else and that something was less than a chicken sitting in the sun on a tub" (72); moreover, he "believed that schoolteacher broke into children what Garner had raised as men" (220). So Paul D's lifelong journey away from doubt and toward self-discovery is a direct consequence of his treatment as a slave. Paul D's description of his value underscores the degree to which slavery fulfilled its dehumanizing project.

Another dehumanizing moment in *Beloved* occurs when schoolteacher and the rest of the posse track Sethe and her family; the humans are objectified—"a crazy old nigger," "a nigger woman," "the old nigger boy," "creatures"—and the dogs are distinguished by their names—"Chipper" and "Samson" (149–50). In a world where beasts are treated like humans, the slave's narrative acquires more than a quest for survival in a physically hostile environment; it acquires the urgency of the spiritual survivability of the enslaved, and, by inverting the proverbial hierarchy of the animal kingdom, the narrative exposes the perverseness of slavery and its aftermath, especially when we read *Beloved* antecedent to *Song of Solomon*. Add to these the perverseness of white lynchings and, like that of Morrison's father, Stamp Paid's response acquires profound moral implications: "What *are* these people. You tell me, Jesus. What *are* they?" (180).

What is evident in these examples and elsewhere in Morrison's fiction is that, from a white perspective, morality takes on a different hue in the context of black-white relations. Examples from other novels come to mind. In *Sula*, Jude Green and the other men in Medallion define manhood in the context of the work denied or the work they are compelled to perform, both conditions attributable to white men who control the jobs. "It was after he stood in line for six days running and saw the gang boss pick out thin-armed white boys from the Virginia hills and the bull-necked Greeks and Italians and heard over and over, 'Nothing else today. Come back tomorrow,' that he got the message," that because he was black he need not apply. "So it was rage, rage and a determination to take on a man's role anyhow that made him press Nel about settling down. He needed some of his appetite filled, some posture of adulthood recognized, but mostly he wanted someone to care about his hurt, to care very deeply" (82). In a patriarchal economy where a man's work is measured by muscle and the size of his pay check, Jude "wanted the heavy work shoes and the camaraderie of the road men" and a "limp" to identify him as one who had "built" the River Road (81–82). The narrative suggests that Jude, in keeping with the prevailing white myth of black manhood, must define his self-worth mainly by his sexuality. Similarly, Paul D believes that, in order to "document his manhood," he must impregnate Sethe—"I want you pregnant" (*Beloved* 128). These men know that in the larger world a white man is expected to acquire money and stability before marriage, but for a black male, if we accept Jude or Paul as the antithetical black male, sexual liaison with a woman determines stability. With Nel, Jude "was head of a household pinned to an unsatisfactory job of necessity. The two of them was one Jude" (*Sula* 82). Without Nel, Jude regards himself as half or less than a man. Ultimately, Jude's frustrated manhood and the community's outrage at the diminishment of their self-worth, signified by the unfinished tunnel, are vindicated, albeit perversely, when they storm the tunnel "to wipe from the face of the earth the work of the thin-armed Virginia boys . . . and the knife-faced men who waved the leaf-dead promise" (161–62). The outcome is tragic, because many of them die and what is left of the community will soon be dispersed and dismantled for a white golf course. Does the outcome suggest that fighting back is futile? Is it better to fight for the rightness of an idea than to suffer in silence?

It is important to remember that Morrison's moral landscape also entails black racism and embraces an ethic of difference that also indicts blacks. It is equally important in this context to remember the racist philosophies of the "Days" (*Song of Solomon*) and the patriarchs in Ruby (*Paradise*). Terry Otten, in his analysis of Morrison's treatment of good and evil, observes that her "fictions are not simplistic polemics on the viciousness generated by white society," but they "penetrate the characters themselves, exposing their capacity for cowardice and corruption" (5). There are notable examples of what I would call black-on-black "crimes of the heart," or what is best expressed by Claudia in her description of the black community's displacement of its self-hatred onto Pecola, its most vulnerable member: "We honed our egos on her, padded our characters with her frailty, and yawned in the fantasy of our strength" (*Bluest Eye* 159). The textual "we" indirectly implicates the reader for what happened to Pecola.

Consider Macon Dead's willingness to evict Guitar's family because the grandmother uses the rent money for food: "Babies can't make it without nothing to put in their stomachs." Macon is unmoved by the children's hunger or the plight of an old woman: "Can they make it in the street, Mrs. Bains? That's where they gonna be if you don't figure out how to get me my money." Mrs. Bains's answer—"No, sir. They can't make in the street. We need both, I reckon. Same as yours"—is a challenge to Macon's humanity and evokes an unconscionable retort: "Then you better rustle it up, Mrs. Bains. You got . . . Saturday coming." There is no question about Macon's rigid resolve: "Not Sunday. Not Monday, Saturday" (*Song of Solomon* 21). Macon's attitude has a lasting effect on Guitar and becomes part of his accumulated anger toward white people, no doubt, because of Macon's bourgeois values and insensitivity toward his poor black tenants.

In *Tar Baby*, Jadine's callousness toward her elderly relatives' physical decline is expressed by her aunt: "I stand on my feet thirty years so she wouldn't have to"—a sacrifice rewarded with "some shoes I can't wear" and "a dress I shouldn't." The uncle underscores the issue: "Old black people must be a worrisome thing to the young ones these days" (283).

Another instance of a black-on-black crime of the heart occurs in *Beloved* in the community's jealous refusal to warn Baby Suggs's family about the approaching slave catchers: "Nobody sent a fleet-footed son to cut 'cross a field soon as they saw the four horses in town," "not anybody ran down or to Bluestone Road to say some new whitefolks with the Look just rode in." According to Stamp Paid, the community is collusive, jealousy notwithstanding, in the resulting tragedy since their "meanness . . . let them stand aside, or pay no attention" (157). Stamp Paid, like Jadine's relatives, verbalizes the reprehensible deed.

At other times the deeds speak for themselves, as in *Jazz* when Violet describes a family's eviction. Contemplating her neurosis in the context of her mother's, Violet recalls the psychological toll of her father's desertion and the eviction on the mother and on Violet herself, since she is worried that she may be like her mother:

> She didn't want to be like that . . . sipping boiled coffee from a white china cup as long as it was there, and pretending to sip it when it was gone; waiting for morning when men came, talking low as though nobody was there but themselves, and picked around in our things, lifting out what they wanted—what was theirs, they said, although we cooked in it, washed sheets in it, sat on it, ate off of it. That was after they had hauled away the plow, the scythe, the mule, the sow, the churn and the butter press. . . . When they got to the table where our mother sat nursing an empty cup, they took the table out from under her and then, while she sat there alone, and all by herself like, cup in hand, they came back and

tipped the chair she sat in. She didn't jump up right away, so they shook it bit and since she stayed seated—looking ahead at nobody—they just tipped her out of it the way you get the cat off the seat if you don't want to touch it or pick it up in your arms. You tip it forward and it lands on the floor. (97–98)

Violet slips in a brief critique, but, for the most part, the litany of details is self-revelatory: "No harm done if it's a cat because it has four legs. But a person, a woman, might fall forward or just stay there a minute looking at the cup, stronger than she is, unbroken at least and lying a bit beyond her hand. Just out of reach" (98). The scene has multiple frames of reference within and beyond Morrison's oeuvre. While Violet's description recalls Paul D and the rooster, or the pregnant Pauline Breedlove and Sethe being compared to a mare about to foal, or Macon Dead's eviction of the Bains family, it also reiterates, in its catalog of the family's possessions, the eviction scene in Ralph Ellison's *Invisible Man*.[8] Violet, while cataloging the family's property, reveals a great deal about the family's life, a life of industry and self-sufficiency. It is, however, the evictors' behavior toward the mother that screams its moral turpitude. In comparing the men who tip her mother from the chair to someone repulsed by the thought of touching or holding a cat, Violet not only captures their callousness; she also exposes their inhumanity.

The foregoing examples attest to the centrality of the ethics of responsibility in Morrison's oeuvre. Morrison's faith in humanity and in the perdurability of African Americans is evidenced by her unswerving attempts at chronicling the power of the African American spirit through her own reflective vision. Morrison's work shows that, despite the laws and practices that rendered black people less than human or designated them as second-class citizens, black people functioned in the face of dehumanizing conditions—and they continue to act at this moment in history out of a deep conviction that they are not only human but are deserving of human rights and equality of opportunities. Morrison's fiction systematically destabilizes the various forms of difference—de jure and de facto: separate-but-(un)equal doctrine, aesthetic positions, dogma, physical limitations, and negative inscriptions—and uses these dualities and dialectics to reshape our consciousness and excite our moral sensibilities.

NOTES

Chapter 1: "Who Will Play with Jane?"

1. For a discussion of Sula as an atypical black woman, see Spillers, "Hateful Passion."

2. For a discussion of this fusion and possessiveness, see Page.

3. For discussions on theories of the reader in narratives, see Bal, Baldick, Genette, Hutcheon, Iser, O'Neill, Prince, and Rimmon-Kenan.

4. From its beginnings, African American literature has dealt with interracial unions. For discussions of sexual unions between black women and white males, see Carby, A. Y. Davis, Fox-Genovese, Sollors, and White. Fiction by African American women writers from Harriet E. Wilson (1859) onward includes such liaisons.

5. In his introduction to *The Aesthetics of Toni Morrison*, Marc C. Conner reminds us that Morrison's fiction is part of a century-long "discourse on the relations between art and politics in African-American literature that is still prevalent today" (xiii).

6. In this volume Gates also acknowledges that numerous critics have recognized this presumed contradiction surrounding Morrison's texts (x).

7. For detailed discussions of Morrison's perspective on *how* she writes, see Tate and Taylor-Guthrie as well as the various other Morrison interviews and lectures.

8. Benjamin (*Illuminations* 83–109) and Ricoeur (*Time and Narrative*, vol. 2) provide some useful strategies for investigating Morrison's poetics. I am particularly persuaded by Ricoeur's notion of "games with time," which are related to what Booth, in "Ethics of Form," has called "clever play with chronology" (108). Also see Bakhtin (84–258), Fleischman (52–93), and Todorov (*Introduction to Poetics* 27–32).

9. Wimmers is persuaded by her observation and analysis of her students as readers. She observes that the "reader takes on various guises, including different critical and theoretical perspectives as well as different identities." To characterize these "different" approaches to reading, Wimmers uses the phrase "frames of reference" (xv).

10. It should be noted that these multiple views of one issue are often the bases for attacks on Morrison's works. See, for example, Bent and Klinghoffer. Ricoeur, in *Time and Narrative*, states, "Every point of view is an invitation to readers to direct their gaze in the same direction as the author or character" (2:99). Todorov's paraphrase of Bakhtin's "dialogic," in *Introduction to Poetics*, aptly applies to Morrison's fictions: "The dialogic is characterized, essentially, by the absence

of a unifying narrative consciousness that would contain the consciousness of all the characters" (65). On the other hand, Trudier Harris contends that Morrison permits "no dichotomy between form and substance, theme and character" (7). To the contrary, I would argue that one salient characteristic of Morrison's fiction is her dichotomies, even within what appears to be a unified whole. For a discussion of these disjunctions in Morrison's fiction, see Page.

11. Marshall comments on the subjectivity of Morrison's characters vis-à-vis the Euro-American community: "We are not allowed to read or envision these communities [the African American communities posited in Morrison's texts] as 'other'; that is, we may not use the humanist subject as white and male as the measuring stick against which all else is measured. Rather we are introduced to difference and multiplicity within a particular community" (10–11). Marshall touches on something very crucial to Morrison's fiction—the assertion of African Americans as subjects of their own narratives and the subjectivity of characters within these narratives.

Rigney, on the other hand, argues, "For Morrison, to recognize the other as one's 'self,' to come to terms with one's own otherness, to enter willingly the forbidden zones of consciousness (and unconsciousness) that lie through and beyond the mirror of gender and race is to become more fully human, more moral, more sane" (2–3).

12. Here, I am also thinking of Hannah, Sula, and Reba, whose attitudes toward sex may be termed "free" and "loose." I am also reminded of Sula's willed attention to her mother's death by fire. For detailed analyses of this gaze, see B. Johnson, Kolmerten, Novak.

13. Rigney suggests that the reader's role is crucial to the reconstruction of Morrison's poetics in so far as "the reader's own dreams, where that which is repressed, contained, becomes consciously expressed" (27). In *Killing Rage,* hooks writes that "for some readers the focus on slavery directs attention away from current situations of racialized trauma or allows them to trivialize contemporary pain." hooks contends that "much of the contemporary nonfiction writing by black scholars . . . downplays the significance of trauma in order to emphasize triumph over adversity" (141–42).

14. Morrison supports this claim when she speaks of "meaning in the world." In her interview with Schappell, Morrison states, "It is not possible for me to be unaware of the incredible violence, the willful ignorance, the hunger for other people's pain." She contends that what gives her a sense of belonging "out in this world" is "what goes on in [her] mind when [she] is writing. Then I belong here, and then all of the things that are disparate and irreconcilable can be useful. I can do the traditional things . . . which is to make order out of chaos. . . . Struggling through the work is extremely important to me—more than publishing it" (95). Morrison's statement echoes Greenblatt's argument that there is a "social presence to the world of the literary text and the social presence of the world in the literary" (5).

15. Morrison also speaks of this connectedness in her essay "Rootedness."

16. Ricoeur's elaborate treatment of narrative brings him to the conclusion that "the reaffirmation of the historical consciousness within the limits of its validity requires in turn the search by individuals and by communities to which they belong for narrative identities" (*Time and Narrative* 3:274).

17. Also see Baldick (200–201), who uses the term "scriptible" as a synonym for "writerly." Baldick translates Barthes's "writerly/scriptible" text as one that "does not have a single 'closed' meaning: instead, it obliges each reader to produce his or her own meanings from its fragmentary or contradictory hints. . . . The writerly text is challengingly 'open,' giving the reader an active role as co-writer, rather than as passive consumer." Prince offers a more concise definition of the writerly text—one that is "triumphantly plural and totally open" (103).

18. Jones's narrator compares this interplay between writer, text, and reader to a jazz composition: "If it be a book, they be reading it and start telling it theyselves whiles they's reading. . . . if they gets to part of the book where I talks about my daddy . . . then they ain't just have to read about my daddy, they can start talking about they own daddy or other people daddy or even they Spiritual Daddy . . . or anyplace in the novel they wants to integrate they own stories of peoples they knows, so they be reading and composing for theyselves, and writing between the lines, and even between the words. . . . they can compose around the themes, but they could still bring they own multiple perspectives everywhere in that novel, and they own freedom" (*Mosquito* 93–94).

19. In the main, my treatment of these modalities in Morrison's fiction is informed by Genette's *Narrative Discourse* and *Narrative Discourse Revisited*. While some critics make no distinctions between perspective and focalization, for purposes of my examination of Morrison's fiction I prefer Genette's formulations of these narrative modes: perspective answers the question "Who perceives?"; focalization, "Where is the focus of perception?"; and voice, "Who speaks?" (*Narrative Discourse Revisited* 64).

20. Hedin attempts to shift the critical debate of African American texts from theme and "pre-generic myths" to ways by which "culturally necessary forms have come to shape black writers' stories." Hedin, in contrast to those who emphasize form and myths, is interested in the ways in which form indicates that the "expression of strong emotion is under firm rational control." He also argues that it is in "form" that African American writers can make an "argument" for the race's position "indirectly and implicitly rather than overtly through content or comment" (37). See also Baker's *Journey Back* and Stepto's *From Behind the Veil*.

21. Spillers, in "Cross-Currents," makes the case for this broader study of African American women writers in conjunction with their contemporaries as well as within the context of Western literary tradition: "For lack of a better word, we could call this project the 'archaeological' since it questions matters of lexis, syntax, and semantics and tries to decide from what common fund of rhetorical legacies (and betrayals?) writers across time and in the same time were drawing" (258).

22. Furman notes that "a consistent thread of philosophical, literary, political, and cultural thought connects [Morrison's] writing" (104).

23. Critics have observed Morrison's depiction of numerous characters with (un)marked bodies and missing parts. Page observes that, in Morrison's fiction, "body parts are frequently missing or torn off . . . bodies are repeatedly violated or invaded" (30–31). Page further notes that "Pilate's lack of a navel, after causing her anguish and alienation, leads to her self-creation of a viable self" (92).

Chapter 2: Playing with Difference

1. Gates, in "Writing 'Race,'" observes that the shared assumption among intellectuals is that race is a "thing, an ineffable quantity, which irresistibly determines the shape and contour of human anatomy" (2–3). Awkward formulates the issue this way: "Race arises as a significant consideration only as a consequence of our engagement with ideologically saturated texts and codes" (*Negotiating Difference* 13).

2. Appiah points out that race has been an important aspect of literary study since the turn of the nineteenth century when it became "important as the theme of a great body of writing in Europe and North America." He further notes that a thematics of race is frequently useful to writers in the constructing of plot (277, 279). Dijk also reminds us that "stories are rich data for guided references about ethnic relations and their cognitive modeling by social members" (*Communicating Racism* 6). While Dijk is concerned with real-life stories and anecdotes humans use in their day-to-day discussions about others outside their racial, ethnic, or national group, his theory can be applied to fictional narratives as well. I am persuaded that Morrison, in "Recitatif," uses Twyla, the narrator, to tell the story of her early friendship and later strained encounters with Roberta in order to show how racism and prejudice undergird our daily conversations.

3. Gates further states that "Race has become the trope of ultimate, irreducible difference between cultures, linguistic groups, or adherents of specific belief systems. . . . Race is the ultimate trope of difference because it is so very arbitrary in its application" ("Writing 'Race'" 5). Spillers, in "'All the Things You Could Be,'" notes that to ignore the political origins of race is "to be politically stupid and endangered." Spillers adds that race is a "complicated figure or metaphoricity that demonstrates the power and danger of difference, that signs and assigns difference as a way to situate social subjects" (137).

4. Abel suggests that Twyla and Roberta saw in Maggie "a hated reminder of their unresponsive mothers." Abel continues along her racial reading of these characters. She states that "Maggie is not 'raced' to Twyla (that is, she is by default white); to Roberta, she is black" ("Black Writing" 472).

5. I am relying on Baldick's definition of the "intentional fallacy," which he defines as "the name given by the American critics W. K. Wimsatt and Monroe C. Beardsley to the widespread assumption that an author's declared or supposed intention in writing a work is the proper basis for deciding on the meaning and value of that work" (110–11).

6. McCullough, in *Black and White Women as Friends*, points to studies that refer to the barriers to cross-racial friendships "rooted in slavery that left a deep inequity" (159).

7. Paul D's thoughts are filtered through the narrator's voice.

8. Spillers, in "Mama's Baby, Papa's Maybe," speaks of this hieroglyphics as the mutilated flesh of enslaved Africans in its "seared, ripped-apartness" (67) resulting from the brutality of slave drivers and slaveholders.

9. Charles Christian, in *Black Saga*, has noted that between 1882 and 1964 "the most heinous" form of "white terrorism" against blacks was lynching. During this period, according to Tuskegee Institute's records, some 4,742 blacks were lynched

(275). Readers familiar with Billie Holiday's and Nina Simone's recordings of "Strange Fruit" may see a connection between the tree on Sethe's back and the trees in the South used for lynching blacks. For a fictional treatment of this theme of "strange fruit," see Lillian Smith; see also Perkins and Stephens for dramatic treatments of this theme. Also see Royster for a study of Ida B. Wells's campaign against lynchings of blacks. For a provocative reading of Sethe's back, see Ledbetter, who contends that the figuration is the "tree of life whose fruit . . . gives knowledge of the gods to those who consume it" (45).

10. Morrison accounts for Sula's idleness and irresponsible behavior by stating, "Had she paints, or clay, or knew the discipline of the dance, or strings; had she anything to engage her tremendous curiosity and her gift for metaphor, she might have exchanged the restlessness and preoccupation with whim for an activity that provided her with all she yearned for" (*Sula* 121). For a detailed analysis of this description of Sula, see Nigro (15–24).

11. For a discussion and redefinition of black women's artistic impulses, see Alice Walker (231–43).

12. Melissa Walker's comments about the difficulties faced by characters in *The Bluest Eye* seeking to escape their blackness are equally applicable to Jadine. Walker writes, "It is . . . a timely novel in its treatment of the tragic consequences for those who attempt to escape blackness by an unrealistic and self-destructive yearning for the symbols . . . and privileges of whiteness or by renouncing their historical identity in order to accommodate to the white world" (50).

13. Ryan reads Jadine's attempt to equate her breasts with those of the phantom "swamp women" as a "sign of Jadine's confusion" and "her perceptions about breasts, a symbol of sustenance, as the implement of destroying . . . what she has become." Ryan points out that Jadine "is not . . . unaware of the fact that these women are trying to reveal and nurture another dimension of her identity" and sees in Jadine's resistance to these phantom women's desire to claim her a fear "that whoever this person might be, she will be faced with the same lack of choice, the same economic and sociopolitical stagnation the swamp women face" (77). Mobley suggests that Jadine, in denying her roots, "risks psychic chaos and alienation from the very sources that would empower her" ("Narrative Dilemma" 291).

14. See Painter for an analysis of Truth as a symbol and a "concoction" (270).

15. I am reminded here of Nel Wright, who makes a similar statement in trying to sever all connections with her parents in the face of her mother's public humiliation by a white train conductor and Nel's concomitant embarrassment. To escape embarrassment and disassociate from her mother's humiliation, Nel asserts an identity free of familial connections: "I'm me. I'm not their daughter. I'm not Nel. I'm me. Me" (*Sula* 28).

16. Jadine's female literary ancestors are, among others, Iola Leroy (Harper, *Iola Leroy*), Helga Crane and Clare Kendry, respectively (Larsen, *Quicksand* and *Passing*), and Angela Murray (Fauset, *Plum Bun*). These women, like Jadine, try to improve their fortunes or escape the delimiting effects of racism by "passing" in a white environment. But they are never fully accepted or integrated into that world, partly because of their guilt engendered by abandoning the black community and/ or their anxieties about exposure or feelings of inadequacy based on their black blood or their choices to live in the white world.

Chapter 3: *"Slips of Sorrow"*

1. See Duvall for autobiographical and contemporaneous elements in Morrison's writings. Although Duvall does not cite Morrison's critical or theoretical library, he does offer a somewhat compelling argument—through the use of Morrison's conversations and interviews—for reading *The Bluest Eye* as part of Morrison's project of "racial self-discovery" (28).

2. I use this pronoun to refer to the *Jazz* narrator because I interpret the narrator as the *book* itself: "Look where your hands are. Now" (229). For further discussions on the identity of this narrator, see Carabi, Matus, and Mayberry. Bouson interprets Morrison's creation of this ambiguous narrator as a device for deflecting readers from the story to the narrative technique. Bouson writes, "If, in following the text's promptings, critic-readers try to solve the mystery of the *Jazz* narrator's identity or focus on the cognitive puzzles and aesthetic pleasures" of the text, they may overlook the "troubling emotional drama at the center of the novel" (189). I would argue that it is possible to combine aesthetic and content analyses without sacrificing either. Bal observes that the "identity of the narrator, the degree to which and the manner in which that identity is indicated in the text, and the choices that are implied lend the text its specific character" (120). The "character" of *Jazz* is not only defined but interpreted by the narrative voice that defines its own role. Yet without content to "contemplate," the narrative is just an empty vessel.

3. For a discussion of this notion of the narrator in *Jazz*, see Doody (253–59). For a discussion on the interplay between the fictional and autobiographical, see Duvall.

4. Consider such characters as Mrs. MacTeer and the three prostitutes (*The Bluest Eye*), Sula and Rochelle (*Sula*), Ella (*Beloved*), and the Convent women (*Paradise*).

5. Freud, in "A Case of Hysteria," describes this condition as "housewife's psychosis" rather than "obsessive neurosis" since the women afflicted with the malady have no "insight into their illness." He uses Dora's description of her mother's preoccupation with house chores as an example, one that, in some respects, describes Geraldine, Pauline, and Helene Wright. Dora's mother "had no understanding of her children's more active interests, and was occupied all day long in cleaning the house with its furniture and in utensils and in keeping them clean—to such an extent as to make it impossible to use or enjoy them" (20). Consider Nel Wright, who "regarded the oppressive neatness of her home with dread" (*Sula* 19).

6. See Stepto, "'Intimate Things,'" in which Morrison concedes that for Pauline's story she chose "two voices, hers and the author's," because of "certain things [Pauline] couldn't know and I had to come in. And then there were certain things the author would say that I wanted in her language—so that there were two things, two voices, which I regarded . . . as a way in which to do something second-best" (222).

7. Weinstein points out that Morrison shows "considerable sympathy" for Pauline's "suffering"; but he also notes that when we no longer hear Pauline's interior voice, we are free to judge her "maternal behavior" (20).

8. Pauline may be read as a precursor to Jadine Childs in *Tar Baby*. Both women have been culturally damaged by rejecting black values for white cultural icons. Both women believe that whites are superior to blacks because whites

have the desirable amenities. In Pauline's case it is the plush homes, with every piece in its proper place, where she can be the queen of glistening pots and pans and fine furniture, and where "her foot flopped around on deep pile carpets, and there was no uneven sound" (*Bluest* 101). For Jadine, it is her "superior" knowledge that Picasso is better than the African sculptor Picasso imitates. For these women, representational figures are better than the real ones upon which they are modeled.

9. For discussions of Morrison's use of mirror imagery, see especially Mori (57–87) and Rigney (38–60).

10. Here Morrison is invoking Cuney's "No Images": "She does not know / Her beauty, / She thinks her brown body / Has no glory" (98).

11. See Ruas for Morrison's discussion on the model for Pecola's character.

12. For a discussion of the pain induced by shame in *The Bluest Eye*, see J. Brooks Bouson.

13. For many blacks the use of the term "jungle," as Rigney construes it, has negative connotations, such as "uncivilized" and "savage." In *Song*, "jungle" has the same resonance as the unarticulated words of the thirty women who come to exercise the demons at 124 Blue Stone Road in *Beloved*.

14. For a discussion of the maieutic function of music in African American women's texts, see Kester, "Blues."

15. See Blassingame, A. Y. Davis, Hartman, hooks (*Ain't I a Woman*), Sterling, and White.

16. Scarry has some remarks on this issue that may well be applicable to Violet's condition. Scarry writes, "A state of consciousness other than pain—such as hunger or desire—will, if deprived of its object, begin to approach the neighborhood of pain, as an acute, unsatisfied hunger or prolonged, objectless longing; conversely, when such a state is given an object, it is itself experienced as a pleasurable and self-eliminating (or more precisely, pleasurable because self-eliminating) physical occurrence." Scarry continues, "The interior state . . . of psychological desire [has] nothing aversive, fearful, or unpleasant about [it] if the person experiencing [it] inhabits a world where . . . a companion is near" (*Body* 166).

17. This need for "a talking cure" through self-articulation calls to mind Hurston's *Their Eyes Were Watching God*, in which Janie Crawford rehearses her traumatic past with her friend Pheoby, who stands in for the insensitive, gossiping community: "If they want to see and know, why don't they come and be kissed? Ah could sit down and tell 'em things. Ah been a delegate to de big 'ssociation of life. De Grand Lodge, de big convention of livin' is just where Ah been dis year and half" (6). Janie later tells Pheoby, "[W]e been kissin'-friends for twenty years, so Ah depend on you from dat standpoint" (7).

18. Violet's need for "a talking cure" also calls to mind Freud and his colleague Josef Breuer's patient Anna O. (Bertha Pappenheim), who is credited with naming the process by which she sought to deal with the psychological trauma of caring for her ill father and her erotic fixation on her physician. See Dianne Hunter, "Hysteria," in which she points out that Pappenheim's physician "overlooked the hostility, anger, guilt, and frustrated sexuality apparent to psychoanalysts" (262). For a detailed discussion of Anna O., see "Fraulein Anna O.," in Freud (2:21–47).

19. Violet's recuperation and reconciliation recall Pauline's failure to revitalize her marriage and reconcile her divided loyalties. Lacking an attentive and

sensitive listener like Alice, Pauline must ponder her condition in solitude and rely on her "Maker" to take care of her.

20. In a conversation with Morrison at Princeton in 1989, I asked her about this neologism. She suggested that I think of a radio with its volume turned to the lowest point, beyond audibility but never turned off. Like the unheard but ever-present voices on the radio, Sethe's memories are always there, just beneath the surface, waiting for someone or something to raise their volume, to render them audible.

Chapter 4: Playing with Narrative

1. See Allen (7), Bent (147), Gray (64), Shields (33), Streitfeld (31), and Thomas (31).

2. I am not persuaded that this sentence is a "throwaway": it signals the intraracial and interracial tensions based on skin color in the novel.

3. Iser, in *The Fictive and the Imaginary*, defines narrative play as a "mode of discovery" that "arises out of the co-existence of the fictive and the imaginary" and that "by opening up spaces to play, the fictive compels the imaginary to take on a form at the same time it acts as a medium for its manifestation." Iser adds that "representation . . . brings about the reciprocal permeation of what is separated by such doublings, and since these doublings are brought about by play, it is play that forms the infrastructure of representation" (xvii–xviii).

4. For this formulation, I am indebted to Bal (78–79).

5. I am borrowing from Hutcheon's *Narcissistic Narrative* (140).

6. In some of her earlier novels, Morrison directly aids the reader in sounding and interpreting names. In *Beloved* and in *Jazz*, for example, she inserts the pronunciation of Sethe's and Felice's names: "Seth-thuh," a woman addressed as "Ma'am" calls out to Sethe (*Beloved* 30). Despite Morrison's efforts, some readers continue to pronounce the name with one syllable. Taking no chances with Felice's name, Morrison lets Felice discuss her own preference for the pronunciation of her name: "'Felice,' he said. And kept on saying it, 'Felice, Felice.' With two syllables, not one like most people do, including my father" (*Jazz* 214). The phrase "two syllables" forestalls any other attempts to pronounce Felice's name, an implied hint to those readers who may wish to give it three syllables. For Morrison, naming and being addressed by one's "proper" name is important and significant. Readers familiar with Morrison's works may recall the circumstances surrounding the naming of the Dead family (*Song of Solomon* 53) and Baby Suggs's insistence on the name by which her husband had addressed her: "He didn't call me 'Jenny.' He called me 'Baby'" (*Beloved* 142). For other references to naming in Morrison's fiction, see *Sula* 18 and *Jazz* 124.

7. For a feminist critique of *Paradise*, see Tally (73–83).

8. Two definitions of "patrician" may metaphorically apply to Patricia: "A person belonging, or reputed to belong, to one of the original families or *gentes* of which the ancient Roman populous [read Haven/Ruby] consisted"; "One versed in the writings of the Fathers; a patristic scholar. *rare*" (*OED Online*, s.v. "patrician").

9. For a detailed analysis of Morrison's equitable rendering of Paul D's and Sethe's stories, see Sitter (17–29).

10. This interplay between narrator and character emulates the interplay between Pauline Breedlove and the narrator (*The Bluest Eye*). The difference, however, is that we have only the narrator's and Pauline's sometimes conflicting versions of the truth. If Patricia is the educated version of Pauline, she represents a merging of body, mind, and aesthetic sensibility—the intellectual who has moved from organizing things (pots, pans, and spices, in Pauline's case) to one whose education and knowledge have provided her with skills to sift through facts and fabrications and theorize from these the meanings of women's lives. Unlike Pauline, who remains an ostracized figure in Lorain, Patricia is an integral part of Ruby.

11. A similar incidence appears in *Song of Solomon* with the birth of Milkman's sisters. In recounting the births, Milkman's father tells him: "I didn't like the notion of his being his own daughter's doctor, especially since she was also my wife. . . . I ended up telling him that nothing could be nastier than a father delivering his own daughter's baby" (71).

12. For a discussion of the problematical reliance on Patricia's perspective, see Wood, "Sensations of Loss," where he states that he wants "to believe . . . that Patricia the schoolteacher is right about the racism of the town" as well as about other details she offers. Wood adds that "if we knew only what Patricia knows about Haven or Ruby we would know almost nothing" (117). I disagree with the latter statement: I think we know much more than we would otherwise know about the politics of Haven and Ruby because of Patricia, despite her biased position.

13. In *The Devil in the Shape of a Woman*, Karlsen notes that in colonial New England women accused of witchcraft were often those who refused "to subordinate themselves to men with institutional authority over them," implying the women's "refusal to subordinate themselves to all persons whom God had placed above them in social hierarchy" and their "lack of deference for [their] male neighbors" (150).

14. Tally, in *Paradise Reconsidered*, reads the novel within the Western genre. She suggests that the novel's opening sentence, the original settlers' migration to the Oklahoma Territory, and Lone's movements—reminiscent of the Lone Ranger, and the narrative's movement between the men's preparation for the raid and Lone's lurking nearby—represent a "meanwhile-back-at-the-ranch" motif: all situate the novel within the Western genre (63–68).

Chapter 5: Reflections on the Ethics of Difference

1. I am partially indebted to Remak, "Between Scylla and Charybdis," when he writes that "aesthetic integration into the literary work—not only (though also) ethical or moral values as such—is a paramount (though not exclusive) factor to ponder when it comes to comprehensive scrutiny of a given work" (25–26).

2. Morrison did not identify her works that use whites as central figures, but it is safe to assume that she had in mind "Recitatif" and *Tar Baby*.

3. In 1981, Morrison staked out her position as a marginal writer by comparing herself to mainstream writers: "I never asked Tolstoy to write for me, a little colored girl in Lorain, Ohio. I never asked Joyce not to mention Catholicism or

the world of Dublin. Never. And I don't know why I should be asked to explain my life to you. We have splendid writers who do that, but I am not one of them. It is that business of being universal, a word hopelessly stripped of meaning for me" (LeClair 124).

4. For further reading see Bordo, L. J. Davis, Hillyer, and Wendell.

5. Carroll erroneously refers to Pecola's relative as her aunt.

6. For a discussion of the physical manifestation of a moral reaction, see Bouson's *Quiet* (91).

7. For a discussion of slaves' use of wit to mock their masters, see Levine's *Black Culture*, which repeats the joke that Morrison plays off: "Yes, suh, Massa, you got less pig now but you sho' got more nigger" (309).

8. In chapter 12 of *Invisible Man*, the narrator describes the black elderly couple's possessions "strewn in the snow like chicken guts." The items include a document indicating that the husband was freed by his slave master on the "sixth day of August 1859," their "cracked dishes and broken down chairs," "a breast pump," "knocking bones," a "dog-eared Bible"—all testaments to the couple's history (272–78).

SELECTED BIBLIOGRAPHY

Works by Toni Morrison

Beloved. New York: Knopf, 1987.

The Big Box (coauthored with Slade Morrison). New York: Jump at the Sun/Hyperion Books for Children, 1999.

Birth of a Nation'hood: Gaze, Script, and Spectacle in the O. J. Simpson Case (coedited with Claudia Brodsky Lacour). New York: Pantheon Books, 1997.

The Bluest Eye. New York: Washington Square Press, 1970.

The Dancing Mind: Speech upon Acceptance of the National Book Foundation Medal for Distinguished Contribution to American Letters on the Sixth of November, Nineteen Hundred and Ninety-six. New York: Knopf, 1997.

"Faulkner and Women." In *Faulkner and Women/Faulkner and Yoknapatawpha, 1985.* Ed. Doreen Fowler and Anne J. Abadie. 295–307. Jackson: University Press of Mississippi, 1986.

"Home." In *The House That Race Built.* Ed. Waheema Lubiano. 1–8. New York: Vintage Books, 1998.

Jazz. New York: Knopf, 1992.

Lecture and Speech of Acceptance, upon the Award of the Nobel Prize for Literature, Delivered in Stockholm on the Seventh of December, Nineteen Hundred and Ninety-Three. New York: Knopf, 1994.

"Memory, Creation, and Writing." *Thought* 59 (December 1984): 385–90.

"The Official Story: Dead Man Golfing." In *Birth of a Nation'hood,* ed. Morrison and Lacour. vii–xxvii.

Paradise. New York: Knopf, 1998.

Playing in the Dark: Whiteness and the Literary Imagination. Cambridge, Mass.: Harvard University Press, 1992.

"Race and Literature." Lecture, University of Chicago, C-SPAN2. 7 March 1997.

"Recitatif." In *Cornerstones: An Anthology of African American Literature.* Ed. Melvin Donalson. 361–74. New York: St Martin's Press, 1996.

"Rootedness: The Ancestor as Foundation." In *Black Women Writers, 1950–1980: A Critical Evaluation.* Ed. Mari Evans. 339–45. New York: Doubleday, 1984.

"The Site of Memory." In *Inventing the Truth: The Art and Craft of Memoir.* Ed. William Zinsser. 101–24. Boston: Houghton Mifflin, 1987.

Song of Solomon. New York: Plume, 1977.

"Strangers." *New Yorker* 74 (12 October 1998): 69–70.

Sula. New York: Plume, 1973.

Tar Baby. New York: Plume, 1981.

"Unspeakable Things Unspoken: The Afro-American Presence in American Literature." *Michigan Quarterly Review* 28 (1989): 1–34.

Critical and Theoretical Texts

Abel, Elizabeth. "Black Writing, White Reading: Race and the Politics of Feminist Interpretation." *Critical Inquiry* 19 (Spring 1993): 470–98.

Abel, Elizabeth, Barbara Christian, and Helene Moglen, eds. *Female Subjects in Black and White: Race, Psychoanalysis, Feminism.* Berkeley: University of California Press, 1997.

Adell, Sandra. *Double-Consciousness/Double Bind: Theoretical Issues in Twentieth-Century Black Literature.* Urbana: University of Illinois Press, 1994.

Allen, Brooke. "The Promised Land." *New York Times Book Review,* 11 January 1998, 6–7.

Appiah, Kwame Anthony. "The Conservation of 'Race.'" *Black American Literature Forum* 23 (1989): 37–60.

———. "Race." In *Critical Terms for Literary Study.* Ed. Frank Lentricchia and Thomas McLaughlin. 274–87. Chicago: University of Chicago Press, 1995.

———. "The Uncompleted Argument: Du Bois and the Illusion of Race." In *"Race," Writing, and Difference.* Ed. Henry Louis Gates Jr. 21–37. Chicago: University of Chicago Press, 1985.

Awkward, Michael. *Inspiring Influences: Tradition, Revision, and Afro-American Women's Novels.* New York: Columbia University Press, 1989.

———. *Negotiating Difference: Race, Gender, and the Politics of Positionality.* Chicago: University of Chicago Press, 1995.

Baker, Houston A., Jr. *The Journey Back: Issues in Black Literature and Criticism.* Chicago: University of Chicago Press, 1980.

Baker, Houston A., Jr., and Denise Redmond, eds. *Afro-American Literary Studies in the 1990s.* Chicago: University of Chicago Press, 1989.

Bakerman, Jane. "The Seams Can't Show: An Interview with Toni Morrison." In *Conversations with Toni Morrison.* Ed. Danille Taylor-Guthrie. 30–42. Jackson: University Press of Mississippi, 1994.

Bakhtin, Mikhail M. *The Dialogic Imagination: Four Essays.* Ed. Michael Holquist. Trans. Caryl Emerson and Michael Holquist. Austin: University of Texas Press, 1981.

Bal, Mieke. *Narratology: Introduction to the Theory of Narrative.* Toronto: University of Toronto Press, 1985.

Baldick, Chris. *The Concise Oxford Dictionary of Literary Terms.* New York: Oxford University Press, 1990.

Baldwin, James. *Go Tell It on the Mountain.* New York: Dell, 1953.

Barksdale, Richard K. "Castration Symbolism in Recent Black American Fiction." *CLA Journal* 29 (1986): 400–413.

Barthes, Roland. *S/Z.* Trans. Richard Miller and Richard Howard. New York: Hill and Wang, 1974.

Bell-Scott, Patricia, et al., eds. *Double Stitch: Black Women Write about Mothers and Daughters.* Boston: Beacon Press, 1991.

Benjamin, Jessica. *Like Subjects, Love Objects: Essays on Recognition and Sexual Difference.* New Haven, Conn.: Yale University Press, 1995.

Benjamin, Walter. *Illuminations.* Trans. Harry Zohn. New York: Schocken Books, 1969.

Bennett, Andrew, ed. *Readers and Reading.* London: Longman, 1995.

Bent, Geoffrey. "Less Than Divine: Toni Morrison's *Paradise.*" *Southern Review* 35 (Winter 1999): 145–49.

Bhabha, Homi K. *The Location of Culture.* New York: Routledge, 1994.

Bjork, Patrick Bryce. *The Novels of Toni Morrison: The Search for Self and Place within the Community.* New York: Lang, 1992.

Blassingame, John, ed. *Slave Testimony: Two Centuries of Letters, Speeches, Interviews, and Autobiographies.* Baton Rouge: Louisiana State University Press, 1977.

Bloom, Harold. *How to Read and Why.* New York: Scribner, 2000.

———, ed. *Toni Morrison.* New York: Chelsea House, 1990.

———, ed. *Toni Morrison's "Sula."* Philadelphia: Chelsea House, 1999.

Bontemps, Arna, ed. *American Negro Poetry.* New York: Hill and Wang, 1963.

Booth, Wayne C. "The Ethics of Form: Taking Flight with *The Wings of the Dove.*" In *Understanding Narrative.* Ed. James Phelan and Peter J. Rabinowitz. 99–135. Columbus: Ohio State University Press, 1994.

Bordo, Susan. *Unbearable Weight: Feminism, Western Culture, and the Body.* Berkeley: University of California Press, 1993.

Boudreau, Kristin. "Pain and the Unmaking of the Self in Toni Morrison's *Beloved.*" *Contemporary Literature* 36 (1995): 447–65.

Bouson, J. Brooks. *Quiet as It's Kept: Shame, Trauma, and Race in the Novels of Toni Morrison.* Albany: State University of New York Press, 2000.

Bowman, Diane K. "Flying High: The American Icarus in Morrison, Roth, and Updike." *Perspectives on Contemporary Literature* 8 (1982): 10–17.

Bruck, Peter. "Returning to One's Roots: The Motif of Searching and Flying in Toni Morrison's *Song of Solomon.*" In *The Afro-American Novel since 1960.* Ed. Peter Bruck and Wolfgang Karrer. 289–305. Amsterdam: Grunder, 1982.

Bruck, Peter, and Wolfgang Karrer, eds. *The Afro-American Novel since 1960.* Amsterdam: Grunder, 1982.

Butler-Evans, Elliott. *Race, Gender, and Desire: Narrative Strategies in the Fiction of Toni Cade Bambara, Toni Morrison, and Alice Walker.* Philadelphia: Temple University Press, 1989.

Byerman, Keith E. "Beyond Realism." In *Toni Morrison: Critical Perspectives Past and Present.* Ed. Henry Louis Gates Jr. and K. A. Appiah. 100–125. New York: Amistad, 1993.

Cade, Toni, ed. *The Black Woman.* New York: Signet, 1970.

Caminero-Santangelo, Marta. *The Madwoman Can't Speak; or, Why Insanity Is Not Subversive.* Ithaca, N.Y.: Cornell University Press, 1998.

Carabi, Angels. "Toni Morrison." *Belles Lettres: A Review of Books by Women* 10 (1995): 40–43.

Carby, Hazel. *Reconstructing Womanhood: The Emergence of the Afro-American Woman Novelist.* New York: Oxford University Press, 1987.

Carroll, Noël. "Art, Narrative, and Moral Understanding." In *Aesthetics and Ethics: Essays at the Intersection.* Ed. Jerrold Levinson. 126–60. Cambridge: Cambridge University Press, 1998.

Christian, Barbara. "The Contemporary Fables of Toni Morrison." In *Toni Mor-*

rison: Critical Perspectives Past and Present. Ed. Henry Louis Gates Jr. and K. A. Appiah. 59–99. New York: Amistad, 1993.

Christian, Charles. *Black Saga: The African American Experience.* Boston: Houghton Mifflin, 1995.

Collins, Patricia Hill. "The Meaning of Motherhood in Black Mother-Daughter Relationships." In *Double Stitch: Black Women Write about Mothers and Daughters.* Ed. Patricia Bell-Scott et al. 42–60. Boston: Beacon Press, 1991.

Conboy, Katie, Nadia Medina, and Sarah Stanbury, eds. *Writing on the Body: Female Embodiment and Feminist Theory.* New York: Columbia University Press, 1997.

Conner, Marc C. "From the Sublime to the Beautiful: The Aesthetic Progression of Toni Morrison." In *The Aesthetics of Toni Morrison,* ed. Conner. 40–76.

———, ed. *The Aesthetics of Toni Morrison: Speaking the Unspeakable.* Jackson: University Press of Mississippi, 2000.

Cook, Ann. "Black Pride? Some Contradictions." In *The Black Woman.* Ed. Toni Cade. 149–61. New York: Signet, 1970.

Culler, Jonathan. *Structuralist Poetics: Structuralism, Linguistics, and the Study of Literature.* Ithaca, N.Y.: Cornell University Press, 1975.

Cuney, Waring. "No Images." In *American Negro Poetry.* Ed. Arna Bontemps. 98–99. New York: Hill and Wang, 1963.

Darling, Marsha. "In the Realm of Responsibility: A Conversation with Toni Morrison." *Women's Review of Books* 5 (March 1988): 8–9.

Darnton, John. "In Sweden, Proof of the Power of Words." *New York Times,* 8 December 1993, C17, C20.

David, Ron. *Toni Morrison Explained: A Reader's Road Map to the Novels.* New York: Random House, 2000.

Davis, Angela Y. *Women, Race, and Class.* New York: Random House, 1981.

Davis, Lennard J. *Enforcing Normalcy: Disability, Deafness, and the Body.* London: Verso, 1995.

de Lauretis, Teresa, ed. *Feminist Studies, Critical Studies.* Bloomington: Indiana University Press, 1986.

Demetrakopoulos, Stephanie A. "The Interdependence of Men's and Women's Individuation." In *New Dimensions of Spirituality: A Biracial and Bicultural Reading of the Novels of Toni Morrison.* Ed. Karla F. C. Holloway and Stephanie A. Demetrakopoulos. 85–99. New York: Greenwood Press, 1987.

Diedrich, Maria, Henry Louis Gates Jr., and Carl Pedersen, eds. *Black Imagination and the Middle Passage.* New York: Oxford University Press, 1999.

Dijk, Teun A. van. *Communicating Racism: Ethnic Prejudice in Thought and Talk.* Newbury Park, Calif.: Sage Publications, 1987.

———. *Elite Discourse and Racism.* Newbury Park, Calif.: Sage Publications, 1993.

Dimock, Wai-Chee. "Feminism, New Historicism, and the Reader." In *Readers and Reading.* Ed. Andrew Bennett. 112–31. London: Longman, 1995.

Donalson, Melvin, ed. *Cornerstones: An Anthology of African American Literature.* New York: St Martin's Press, 1996.

Doody, Terrence. *Among Other Things: A Description of the Novel.* Baton Rouge: Louisiana State University Press, 1998.

Du Bois, W. E. B. *The Souls of Black Folk.* New York: Penguin, 1989.

Dufault, Roseanna Lewis. *Metaphors of Identity: The Treatment of Childhood in Selected Québécois Novels.* Toronto: Associated University Presses, 1991.

Duvall, John N. *The Identifying Fictions of Toni Morrison: Modernist and Postmodern Blackness.* New York: Palgrave, 2000.

Early, Gerald, ed. *Lure and Loathing: Essays on Race, Identity, and the Ambivalence of Assimilation.* New York: Penguin, 1993.

Ellison, Ralph. *Invisible Man.* New York: Vintage, 1996.

Emerson, Ralph W. "Self-Reliance." In *The Harper American Literature.* Ed. Donald McQuade et al. 2d ed. 2 vols. 1:143–60. New York: HarperCollins, 1994.

Evans, Mari, ed. *Black Women Writers, 1950–1980: A Critical Evaluation.* New York: Doubleday, 1984.

Fabre, Genevieve. "Genealogical Archeology; or, The Quest for Legacy in Toni Morrison's *Song of Solomon.*" In *Critical Essays on Toni Morrison.* Ed. Nellie McKay. 105–14. Boston: G. K. Hall, 1988.

Fanon, Frantz. *Black Skin, White Masks.* Trans. Charles Lam Markmann. New York: Grove Weidenfeld, 1967.

———. *The Wretched of the Earth.* Trans. Constance Farrington. New York: Grove Weidenfeld, 1963.

Fauset, Jessie Redmon. *Plum Bun.* Boston: Beacon Press, 1987.

Feelings, Tom. "Middle Passage." Lecture and slide show. Shrine of the Black Madonna, Houston, Tex. 29 October 1995.

Fleischman, Suzanne. *Tense and Narrativity: From Medieval Performance to Modern Fiction.* Austin: University of Texas Press, 1990.

Fowler, Doreen, and Anne J. Abadie, eds. *Faulkner and Women/Faulkner and Yoknapatawpha, 1985.* Jackson: University Press of Mississippi, 1986.

Fox-Genovese, Elizabeth. *Within the Plantation Household: Black and White Women of the Old South.* Chapel Hill: University of North Carolina Press, 1988.

French, Marilyn. "Is There a Feminist Perspective?" In *Aesthetics in Feminist Perspective.* Ed. Hilde Hein and Carolyn Korsmeyer. 68–76. Bloomington: Indiana University Press, 1993.

Freud, Sigmund. "Fragment of an Analysis of a Case of Hysteria (1905 [1901])." In *The Standard Edition of the Complete Psychological Works of Sigmund Freud*, 7:7–122.

———. "Fräulein Anna O." In *The Standard Edition of the Complete Psychological Works of Sigmund Freud*, 2:21–47.

———. "On Narcissism: An Introduction." In *A General Selection from the Works of Sigmund Freud.* Ed. John Rickman. 104–23. New York: Doubleday, 1957.

———. *The Standard Edition of the Complete Psychological Works of Sigmund Freud.* Trans. James Strachey et al. 24 vols. London: Hogarth Press and the Institute for Psycho-Analysis, 1953.

———. "Three Essays on the Theory of Sexuality." In *The Standard Edition of the Complete Psychological Works of Sigmund Freud*, 7:135–243.

Furman, Jan. *Toni Morrison's Fiction.* Columbia: University of South Carolina Press, 1996.

Furst, Lilian R., ed. *Women Healers and Physicians: Climbing the Long Hill.* Lexington: University Press of Kentucky, 1997.

Gates, Henry Louis, Jr. *The Signifying Monkey: A Theory of Afro-American Literature.* New York: Oxford University Press, 1988.

―――. "Writing 'Race' and the Difference It Makes." In *"Race," Writing, and Difference*, ed. Gates. 1–20.

―――, ed. *"Race," Writing, and Difference*. Chicago: University of Chicago Press, 1985.

Gates, Henry Louis, Jr., and K. A. Appiah, eds. *Toni Morrison: Critical Perspectives Past and Present*. New York: Amistad, 1993.

Genette, Gérard. *Narrative Discourse*. Trans. Jane E. Lewin. Ithaca, N.Y.: Cornell University Press, 1980.

―――. *Narrative Discourse Revisited*. Trans. Jane E. Lewin. Ithaca, N.Y.: Cornell University Press, 1988.

George, Rosemary M. *The Politics of Home: Postcolonial Relocations and Twentieth-Century Fiction*. New York: Cambridge University Press, 1996.

Gibson, Donald B. "Text and Countertext in Toni Morrison's *The Bluest Eye*." *LIT* 1 (1989): 19–32.

Gilroy, Paul. *The Black Atlantic: Modernity and Double Consciousness*. Cambridge, Mass.: Harvard University Press, 1993.

Gray, Paul. "Paradise Found." *Time*, 19 January 1998, 63–68.

Greenblatt, Stephen, *Renaissance Self-Fashioning: From More to Shakespeare*. Chicago: University of Chicago Press, 1980.

Gresson, Aaron David, III. *The Recovery of Race in America*. Minneapolis: University of Minnesota Press, 1995.

Grewal, Gurleen. *Circles of Sorrow, Lines of Struggle: The Novels of Toni Morrison*. Baton Rouge: Louisiana State University Press, 1998.

Grier, William H., and Price M. Cobbs. *Black Rage*. New York: Bantam, 1968.

Harding, Wendy, and Jacky Martin. *A World of Difference: An Inter-Cultural Study of Toni Morrison's Novels*. Westport, Conn.: Greenwood Press, 1994.

Harper, Frances E. W. *Iola Leroy*. 1892. Boston: Beacon Press, 1987.

Harper, Michael S., and Robert B. Stepto, eds. *Chant of Saints: A Gathering of Afro-American Literature, Art, and Scholarship*. Urbana: University of Illinois Press, 1979.

Harris, Trudier. *Fiction and Folklore: The Novels of Toni Morrison*. Knoxville: University of Tennessee Press, 1993.

Hartman, Saidya V., ed. *Scenes of Subjection: Terror, Slavery, and Self-Making in Nineteenth-Century America*. New York: Oxford University Press, 1997.

Hedin, Raymond. "The Structure of Emotion in Black American Fiction." *Novel* 16 (Fall 1982): 50.

Hein, Hilde, and Carolyn Korsmeyer, eds. *Aesthetics in Feminist Perspective*. Bloomington: Indiana University Press, 1993.

Heinze, Denise. *The Dilemma of "Double Consciousness": Toni Morrison's Novels*. Athens: University of Georgia Press, 1993.

Henderson, Mae G. "Speaking in Tongues: Dialogics, Dialectics, and the Black Writer's Literary Tradition." In *Changing Our Own Words: Essays on Criticism, Theory, and Writing*. Ed. Cheryl A. Wall. 16–37. New Brunswick, N.J.: Rutgers University Press, 1989.

Hillyer, Barbara. *Feminism and Disability*. Norman: University of Oklahoma Press, 1993.

Hine, Darlene Clark. "'In the Kingdom of Culture': Black Women and the Intersection of Race, Gender, and Class." In *Lure and Loathing: Essays on Race*,

Identity, and the Ambivalence of Assimilation. Ed. Gerald Early. 337–51. New York: Penguin, 1993.

Hirsch, Marianne. "Knowing Their Names: Toni Morrison's *Song of Solomon*." In *New Essays on "Song of Solomon."* Ed. Valerie Smith. 69–92. Cambridge: Cambridge University Press, 1995.

Holloway, Karla F. C., and Stephanie A. Demetrakopoulos. *New Dimensions of Spirituality: A Biracial and Bicultural Reading of the Novels of Toni Morrison.* New York: Greenwood Press, 1987.

hooks, bell. *Ain't I a Woman: Black Women and Feminism.* Boston: South End, 1981.

———. *Killing Rage: Ending Racism.* New York: Henry Holt, 1995.

———. *Yearning: Race, Gender, and Cultural Politics.* Boston: South End, 1990.

Hunt, Patricia. "War and Peace: Transfigured Categories and the Politics of *Sula*." *African American Review* 27 (1993): 443–59.

Hunter, Dianne. "Hysteria, Psychoanalysis, and Feminism: The Case of Anna O." In *Writing on the Body: Female Embodiment and Feminist Theory.* Ed. Katie Conboy, Nadia Medina, and Sarah Stanbury. 257–76. New York: Columbia University Press, 1997.

Hurston, Zora Neale. *Their Eyes Were Watching God.* New York: Harper and Row, 1990.

Hutcheon, Linda. *Narcissistic Narrative: The Metafictional Paradox.* New York: Methuen, 1980.

———. *A Poetics of Postmodernism: History, Theory, Fiction.* New York: Routledge, 1988.

———. *A Politics of Postmodernism.* New York: Routledge, 1989.

Iser, Wolfgang. *The Act of Reading: A Theory of Aesthetic Response.* Baltimore: Johns Hopkins University Press, 1978.

———. "Do I Write for an Audience?" *PMLA* 115 (2000): 310–14.

———. *The Fictive and the Imaginary: Charting Literary Anthropology.* Baltimore: Johns Hopkins University Press, 1993.

———. *The Implied Reader: Patterns of Communication in Prose Fiction from Bunyan to Beckett.* Baltimore: Johns Hopkins University Press, 1974.

———. "Interaction between Text and Reader." In *The Reader in the Text: Essays on Audience and Interpretation.* Ed. Susan R. Sulieman and Inge Crosman. 106. Princeton, N.J.: Princeton University Press, 1980.

Jacobs, Harriet A. *Incidents in the Life of a Slave Girl, Written by Herself.* Cambridge, Mass.: Harvard University Press, 1987.

Jaffrey, Zia. "The Salon Interview: Toni Morrison." Transcript. 1–9. <http://www.salon.com/books/int/1998/cov_si_02int.html>. 2 February 1998.

James, Rose, and Louis S. Nye, eds. *The Bluest Eye and Sula* [electronic text]. Lincoln, Nebr.: Cliffs Notes, 1997.

Johnson, Barbara. "'Aesthetic' and 'Rapport' in Toni Morrison's *Sula*." *Textual Practice* 7 (1993): 165–72.

Johnson, Charles. *Being and Race: Black Writing since 1970.* Bloomington: Indiana University Press, 1988.

Johnson, Dianne. *Telling Tales: The Pedagogy and Promise of African American Literature for Youth.* Westport, Conn.: Greenwood Press, 1990.

Jones, Gayl. *Corregidora.* Boston: Beacon Press, 1986.

———. *Eva's Man.* 1976. Boston: Beacon Press, 1987.

———. *Mosquito.* Boston: Beacon Press, 1999.

Jost, François, and Melvin J. Friedman, eds. *Aesthetics and the Literature of Ideas.* Newark: University of Delaware Press, 1990.

Kakutani, Michiko. "Worthy Women, Unredeemable Men." *New York Times,* 6 January 1998, E8.

Karlsen, Carol F. *The Devil in the Shape of a Woman: Witchcraft in Colonial New England.* New York: W. W. Norton, 1998.

Kearns, Michael. *Rhetorical Narratology.* Lincoln: University of Nebraska Press, 1999.

Kester, Gunilla T. "The Blues, Healing, and Cultural Representation in Contemporary African American Women's Literature." In *Women Healers and Physicians: Climbing the Long Hill.* Ed. Lilian R. Furst. 114–27. Lexington: University Press of Kentucky, 1997.

———. *Writing the Subject: "Bildung" and the African American Text.* New York: Peter Lang, 1995.

Khayati, Abdellatif. "Representation, Race, and the 'Language' of the Ineffable in Toni Morrison's Narrative." *African American Review* 33 (1999): 313–24.

King, Joyce, E. "Dysconscious Racism: Ideology, Identity, and the Miseducation of Teachers." *Journal of Negro Education* 60 (1991): 9–27.

Kismaric, Carole, and Marvin Heiferman. *Growing Up with Dick and Jane: Learning and Living the American Dream.* San Francisco: Collins, 1996.

Klinghoffer, David. "Black Madonna." *National Review* 9 (February 1998): 30–32.

Kolmerten, Carol A., Stephen M. Ross, and Judith Bryant Wittenberg, eds. *Unflinching Gaze: Morrison and Faulkner Re-Envisioned.* Jackson: University Press of Mississippi, 1997.

Kubitschek, Missy Dehn. *Toni Morrison: A Reader's Companion.* Westport, Conn.: Greenwood Press, 1998.

Larsen, Nella. *Passing.* New Brunswick, N.J.: Rutgers University Press, 1986.

———. *Quicksand.* New Brunswick, N.J.: Rutgers University Press, 1986.

LeClair, Thomas. "The Language Must Not Sweat: A Conversation with Toni Morrison." In *Conversations with Toni Morrison.* Ed. Danille Taylor-Guthrie. 119–28. Jackson: University Press of Mississippi, 1994.

Ledbetter, Mark. *Victims and the Postmodern; or, Doing Violence to the Body: An Ethic of Reading and Writing.* New York: St. Martin's Press, 1996.

Lee, Rachel. "Missing Peace in Toni Morrison's *Sula* and *Beloved.*" *African American Review* 28 (1994): 571–83.

Lentricchia, Frank, and Thomas McLaughlin, eds. *Critical Terms for Literary Study.* Chicago: University of Chicago Press, 1995.

Levine, Lawrence W. *Black Culture and Black Consciousness: Afro-American Folk Thought from Slavery to Freedom.* New York: Oxford University Press, 1977.

Levinson, Jerrold, ed. *Aesthetics and Ethics: Essays at the Intersection.* Cambridge: Cambridge University Press, 1998.

Lidinsky, April. "Prophesying Bodies: Calling for a Politics of Collectivity in Toni Morrison's *Beloved.*" In *The Discourse of Slavery: Aphra Behn to Toni Morrison.* Ed. Carl Plasa and Betty J. Ring. 191–216. New York: Routledge, 1994.

Lorde, Audre. *Sister Outsider: Essays and Speeches.* Freedom, Calif.: Crossing Press, 1984.

Lubiano, Waheema, ed. *The House That Race Built.* New York: Vintage Books, 1998.

Malinowski, Sharon. "Morrison, Toni." In *Black Writers: A Selection of Sketches from Contemporary Authors.* Ed. Sharon Malinowski. 2d ed. 431–39. Detroit: Gale Research, 1994.

Marshall, Brenda K. *Teaching the Postmodern: Fiction and Theory.* New York: Routledge, 1992.

Martin, Biddy, and Chandra T. Mohanty. "Feminist Politics: What's Home Got to Do with It?" In *Feminist Studies, Critical Studies.* Ed. Teresa de Lauretis. 191–212. Bloomington: Indiana University Press, 1986.

Mascia-Lees, Frances. "Double Liminality and the Black Woman Writer." *American Behavioral Scientist* 31 (1987): 101–14.

Mason, Theodore O., Jr. "The Novelist as Conservator: Stories and Comprehension in Toni Morrison's *Song of Solomon.*" In *Toni Morrison.* Ed. Harold Bloom. 171–88. New York: Chelsea House, 1990.

Matus, Jill. *Toni Morrison.* Manchester, U.K.: Manchester University Press, 1998.

Mayberry, Katherine. "The Problem of the Narrator in Toni Morrison's *Jazz.*" In *Toni Morrison's Fiction: Contemporary Criticism.* Ed. David Middleton. 297–309. New York: Garland, 1997.

McCullough, Mary W. *Black and White Women as Friends: Building Cross-Race Friendships.* Cresskill, N.J.: Hampton Press, 1998.

McDowell, Deborah E. "Boundaries; or, Distant Relations and Close Kin." In *Afro-American Literary Studies in the 1990s.* Ed. Houston A. Baker Jr. and Denise Redmond. 51–77. Chicago: University of Chicago Press, 1989.

McKay, Nellie. "An Interview with Toni Morrison." *Contemporary Literature* 24 (1983): 413–29.

———, ed. *Critical Essays on Toni Morrison.* Boston: G. K. Hall, 1988.

McKay, Nellie Y., and Kathryn Earle, eds. *Approaches to Teaching Toni Morrison's "Beloved."* New York: Modern Language Association, 1997.

McQuade, Donald, et al., eds. *The Harper American Literature.* 2d ed. 2 vols. New York: HarperCollins, 1994.

Middleton, David L., ed. *Toni Morrison's Fiction: Contemporary Criticism.* New York: Garland, 1997.

Miner, Madonne M. "Lady No Longer Sings the Blues: Rape, Madness, and Silence in *The Bluest Eye.*" In *Conjuring: Black Women, Fiction, and Literary Tradition.* Ed. Hortense J. Spillers and Marjorie Pryse. 176–91. Bloomington: Indiana University Press, 1985.

Mitchell, David T., and Sharon L. Snyder, eds. *The Body and Physical Difference: Discourse of Disability.* Ann Arbor: University of Michigan Press, 1997.

Mobley, Marilyn Sanders. "Call and Response: Voice, Community, and Dialogic Structures in Toni Morrison's *Song of Solomon.*" In *New Essays on "Song of Solomon."* Ed. Valerie Smith. 41–68. Cambridge: Cambridge University Press, 1995.

———. *Folk Roots and Mythic Wings in Sarah Orne Jewett and Toni Morrison: The Cultural Function of Narrative.* Baton Rouge: Louisiana State University Press, 1991.

———. "Narrative Dilemma: Jadine as Cultural Orphan in *Tar Baby.*" In *Toni Morrison: Critical Perspectives Past and Present.* Ed. Henry Louis Gates Jr. and K. A. Appiah. 284–92. New York: Amistad, 1993.

Montieth, Sharon. *Advancing Sisterhood? Interracial Friendships in Contemporary Southern Fiction.* Athens: University of Georgia Press, 2000.

Mori, Aoi. *Toni Morrison and Womanist Discourse.* New York: Peter Lang, 1999.

Morris, Willie. "Faulkner's Mississippi." *National Geographic* 175 (March 1989): 313–39.

Moses, Cat. "The Blues Aesthetic in Toni Morrison's *The Bluest Eye.*" *African American Review* 33 (1999): 623–36.

Murine, Anna. "This Side of Paradise." Transcript. Toni Morrison interview with Amazon.com. <http://www.amazon.com/exec/obidos/ts/feature/7651/102-8104692-8375306>. 19 January 1998.

Ngugi wa Thiong'o. *Decolonising the Mind: The Politics of Language in African Literature.* Portsmouth, N.H.: Heinemann, 1986.

Nigro, Marie. "In Search of Self: Frustration and Denial in Toni Morrison's *Sula.*" In *Toni Morrison's "Sula."* Ed. Harold Bloom. 15–24. Philadelphia: Chelsea House, 1999.

"Nobel Prize for Literature 1993—Press Release," 7 October 1993. <http://www.nobel.se/literature/laureates/1993.html>. 19 January 2002.

"Nobel Prize–Winning Author Toni Morrison." 1–9. <http://www.time.com/time/community/transcripts/chattr012198html>. 21 January 1998.

Novak, Philip. "'Circles and Circles of Sorrow': In the Wake of Morrison's *Sula.*" *PMLA* 114 (March 1999): 184–93.

Nussbaum, Martha C. *Love's Knowledge: Essays on Philosophy and Literature.* New York: Oxford University Press, 1990.

O'Neill, Patrick. *Fictions of Discourse: Reading Narrative Theory.* Toronto: University of Toronto Press, 1994.

Otten, Terry. *The Crime of Innocence in the Fiction of Toni Morrison.* Columbia: University of Missouri Press, 1989.

Page, Philip. *Dangerous Freedom: Fusion and Fragmentation in Toni Morrison's Novels.* Jackson: University Press of Mississippi, 1995.

Painter, Nell Irvin. *Sojourner Truth: A Life, a Symbol.* New York: W. W. Norton, 1996.

Pankhurst, Anne. "Recontextualization of Metonymy in Narrative and the Case of Toni Morrison's *Song of Solomon.*" In *Metonymy in Language and Thought.* Ed. Klaus-Ewe Panther and Günter Radden. 385–99. Philadelphia: John Benjamins, 1999.

Panther, Klaus-Ewe, and Günter Radden, eds. *Metonymy in Language and Thought.* Philadelphia: John Benjamins, 1999.

Patterson, Orlando. *The Ordeal of Integration: Progress and Resentment in America's "Racial" Crisis.* Washington, D.C.: Civitas/Counterpoint, 1997.

Perkins, Kathy A., and Judith L. Stephens, eds. *Strange Fruit: Plays on Lynching by American Women.* Bloomington: Indiana University Press, 1998.

Peterson, Nancy J., ed. *Toni Morrison: Critical and Theoretical Approaches.* Baltimore: Johns Hopkins University Press, 1997.

Phelan, James, and Peter J. Rabinowitz. *Understanding Narrative.* Columbus: Ohio State University Press, 1994.

Plasa, Carl, ed. *Toni Morrison: "Beloved"* (critical companion). New York: Columbia University Press, 1998.

Plasa, Carl, and Betty J. Ring., eds. *The Discourse of Slavery: Aphra Behn to Toni Morrison.* New York: Routledge, 1994.

Plimpton, George, ed. *Women Writers at Work: The "Paris Review" Interviews.* New York: Modern Library, 1993.

Porter, James I. Foreword to *The Body and Physical Difference: Discourse of Disability.* Ed. David T. Mitchell and Sharon L. Snyder. xiii–xiv. Ann Arbor: University of Michigan Press, 1997.

Prince, Gerald. *A Dictionary of Narratology.* Lincoln: University of Nebraska Press, 1987.

Rabinowitz, Peter J. *Before Reading: Narrative Conventions and the Politics of Interpretation.* Ithaca, N.Y.: Cornell University Press, 1987.

Raynaud, Claudine. "The Poetics of Abjection in *Beloved.*" In *Black Imagination and the Middle Passage.* Ed. Maria Diedrich, Henry Louis Gates Jr., and Carl Pedersen. 70–85. New York: Oxford University Press, 1999.

Remak, Henry H. H. "Between Scylla and Charybdis: Quality Judgment in Comparative Literature." In *Aesthetics and the Literature of Ideas.* Ed. François Jost and Melvin J. Friedman. 21–33. Newark: University of Delaware Press, 1990.

Rich, Adrienne. *Of Woman Born: Motherhood as Experience and Institution.* New York: W. W. Norton, 1986.

Richards, Graham. *"Race," Racism, and Psychology: Towards a Reflexive History.* New York: Routledge, 1997.

Rickman, John, ed. *A General Selection from the Works of Sigmund Freud.* New York: Doubleday, 1957.

Ricoeur, Paul. *The Rule of Metaphor: Multi-Disciplinary Studies of the Creation of Meaning in Language.* Trans. Robert Czerny with Kathleen McLaughlin and John Costello, S.J. Toronto: University of Toronto Press, 1977.

———. *Time and Narrative.* Trans. Kathleen McLaughlin and David Pellauer. 3 vols. Chicago: University of Chicago Press, 1984–88.

Rigney, Barbara Hill. *The Voices of Toni Morrison.* Columbus: Ohio State University Press, 1991.

Rimmon-Kenan, Shlomith. *Narrative Fiction: Contemporary Poetics.* New York: Methuen, 1983.

Robinson, May, ed. *Beloved* [electronic book]. Lincoln, Nebr.: Cliffs Notes, 1993.

Rose, Charlie. "Toni Morrison Suggests *Paradise* Defined by Inclusion." *Charlie Rose Show.* Public Broadcasting System. Transcript. 19 January 1998.

Royster, Jacqueline Jones, ed. *Southern Horrors and Other Writings: The Anti-Lynching Campaign of Ida B. Wells, 1892–1900.* Boston: Bedford Books, 1997.

Ruas, Charles. "Toni Morrison." In *Conversations with Toni Morrison.* Ed. Danille Taylor-Guthrie. 93–118. Jackson: University Press of Mississippi, 1994.

Ryan, Judylyn S. "Contested Visions/Double-Vision in *Tar Baby.*" In *Toni Morrison: Critical and Theoretical Approaches.* Ed. Nancy J. Peterson. 63–87. Baltimore: Johns Hopkins University Press, 1997.

Scarry, Elaine. *The Body in Pain: The Making and Unmaking of the World.* New York: Oxford University Press, 1985.

———, ed. *Literature and the Body: Essays on Populations and Persons.* Baltimore: Johns Hopkins University Press, 1988.

Schappell, Elissa. "Toni Morrison: The Art of Fiction." *Paris Review* 128 (1993): 83–125.

Shields, Carol. "Heaven on Earth." *Washington Post,* 26 January 1998, 33.

Sitter, Deborah Ayer. "The Making of a Man: Dialogic Meaning in *Beloved.*" *African American Review* 26 (1992): 17–29.

Smith, Lillian. *Strange Fruit.* New York: Reynal and Hitchcock, 1944.

Smith, Valerie, ed. *New Essays on "Song of Solomon."* Cambridge: Cambridge University Press, 1995.

Sollors, Werner, ed. *Interracialism: Black-White Intermarriage in American History, Literature, and Law.* New York: Oxford University Press, 2000.

Spillers, Hortense J. "'All the Things You Could Be by Now, If Sigmund Freud's Wife Was Your Mother': Psychoanalysis and Race." In *Female Subjects in Black and White: Race, Psychoanalysis, Feminism.* Ed. Elizabeth Abel, Barbara Christian, and Helene Moglen. 135–58. Berkeley: University of California Press, 1997.

———. "Cross-Currents, Discontinuities: Black Women's Fiction." In *Conjuring: Black Women, Fiction, and Literary Tradition.* Ed. Hortense J. Spillers and Marjorie Pryse. 249–61. Bloomington: Indiana University Press, 1985.

———. "A Hateful Passion, a Lost Love." In *Toni Morrison.* Ed. Harold Bloom. 27–54. New York: Chelsea House, 1990.

———. "Mama's Baby, Papa's Maybe: An American Grammar Book." *Diacritics* 17 (1987): 65–81.

Spillers, Hortense J., and Marjorie Pryse, eds. *Conjuring: Black Women, Fiction, and Literary Tradition.* Bloomington: Indiana University Press, 1985.

Stepto, Robert B. *From Behind the Veil: A Study of Afro-American Narrative.* Urbana: University of Illinois Press, 1979.

———. "'Intimate Things in Place': A Conversation with Toni Morrison." In *Chant of Saints: A Gathering of Afro-American Literature, Art, and Scholarship.* Ed. Michael S. Harper and Robert B. Stepto. 213–29. Urbana: University of Illinois Press, 1979.

Sterling, Dorothy. *We Are Your Sisters: Black Women in the Nineteenth Century.* New York: W. W. Norton, 1984.

Streitfeld, David. "Morrison Confronts Race by Ignoring It." *Houston Chronicle Zest,* 18 January 1998, 26, 31.

Suleiman, Susan R. "Introduction: Varieties of Audience-Oriented Criticism." In *The Reader in the Text: Essays on Audience and Interpretation.* Ed. Susan R. Suleiman and Inge Crosman. 3–45. Princeton, N.J.: Princeton University Press, 1980.

Suleiman, Susan R., and Inge Crosman, eds. *The Reader in the Text: Essays on Audience and Interpretation.* Princeton, N.J.: Princeton University Press, 1980.

Tally, Justine. *Paradise Reconsidered: Toni Morrison's (Hi)stories and Truths.* Hamburg: Lit, 1999.

Tate, Claudia. "Toni Morrison." In *Black Women Writers at Work,* ed. Tate. 117–31.

———, ed. *Black Women Writers at Work.* New York: Continuum, 1989.

Taussig, Michael. *Mimesis and Alterity: A Particular History of the Senses.* New York: Routledge, 1993.

Taylor-Guthrie, Danille, ed. *Conversations with Toni Morrison.* Jackson: University Press of Mississippi, 1994.

Thomas, Lorenzo. "Great Reward: Author's Wisdom Awaits Readers in *Paradise.*" *Houston Chronicle Zest,* 18 January 1998, 26, 31.

Thomson, Rosemarie Garland. "Disabled Women as Powerful Women in Petry, Morrison, and Lorde: Revising Black Female Subjectivity." In *The Body and Physical Difference: Discourse of Disability.* Ed. David T. Mitchell and Sharon L. Snyder. 240–66. Ann Arbor: University of Michigan Press, 1997.

Todorov, Tzvetan. *Genres in Discourse.* Trans. Catherine Porter. Cambridge: Cambridge University Press, 1990.

———. *Introduction to Poetics.* Trans. Richard Howard. Minneapolis: University of Minnesota Press, 1981.

Tolstoy, Leo. *What Is Art?* Trans. Richard Pevear and Larissa Volokhonsky. New York: Penguin, 1995.

Truth, Sojourner. "Ain't I a Woman?" In *Writing on the Body: Female Embodiment and Feminist Theory.* Ed. Katie Conboy, Nadia Medina, and Sarah Stanbury. 231–32. New York: Columbia University Press, 1997.

Walker, Alice. *In Search of Our Mothers' Gardens.* New York: Harcourt Brace Jovanovich, 1983.

Walker, Melissa. *Down from the Mountaintop: Black Women's Novels in the Wake of the Civil Rights Movement, 1966–1989.* New Haven, Conn.: Yale University Press, 1991.

Wall, Cheryl A., ed. *Changing Our Own Words: Essays on Criticism, Theory, and Writing.* New Brunswick, N.J.: Rutgers University Press, 1989.

Weinstein, Philip M. *What Else But Love: The Ordeal of Race in Faulkner and Morrison.* New York: Columbia University Press, 1996.

Wendell, Susan. *The Rejected Body: Feminist Philosophical Reflections on Disability.* New York: Routledge, 1996.

Wendt, Lana. "Toni Morrison Uncensored." Videorecording. Princeton, N.J.: Films for the Humanities and Sciences, 1998.

West, Cornel. *Race Matters.* Boston: Beacon Press, 1993.

White, Deborah Gray. *Ar'n't I a Woman? Female Slaves in the Plantation South.* New York: W. W. Norton, 1985.

Wilkerson, Margaret B. "The Dramatic Voice in Toni Morrison's Novels." In *Critical Essays on Toni Morrison.* Ed. Nellie McKay. 179–90. Boston: G. K. Hall, 1988.

Wilson, Harriet E. *Our Nig; or, Sketches from the Life of a Free Black, in a Two-Story White House, North.* 1859. New York: Random House, 1983.

Wimmers, Inge Crosman. *Poetics of Reading: Approaches to the Novel.* Princeton, N.J.: Princeton University Press, 1988.

Winfrey, Oprah. *Journey to Beloved.* New York: Hyperion, 1998.

Wood, Michael. "Sensations of Loss." In *The Aesthetics of Toni Morrison: Speaking the Unspeakable.* Ed. Marc C. Conner. 113–24. Jackson: University Press of Mississippi, 2000.

Wong, Shelley. "Transgression as Poesis in *The Bluest Eye.*" In *Toni Morrison.* Ed. Harold Bloom. 139–51. New York: Chelsea House, 1990.

Zinsser, William, ed. *Inventing the Truth: The Art and Craft of Memoir.* Boston: Houghton Mifflin, 1987.

INDEX

Unless otherwise noted, all titles are of works by Toni Morrison.

LUCILLE P. FULTZ, an associate professor of English at Rice University, has been an NEH Fellow, a Mellon Fellow, and the recipient of a Ford Foundation grant. She is a coeditor of *Double Stitch: Black Women Write about Mothers and Daughters* (1991) and has published essays on Toni Morrison.

The University of Illinois Press
is a founding member of the
Association of American University Presses.

Composed in 9.5/12.5 Trump Mediaeval
by Celia Shapland
for the University of Illinois Press
Manufactured by Thomson-Shore, Inc.

University of Illinois Press
1325 South Oak Street
Champaign, IL 61820-6903
www.press.uillinois.edu